BEACH

CHIC

NICS

POOL

D OCEAN

RTS

SUMMER

THE
SUMMERTIME
ANYTIME
COOKBOOK

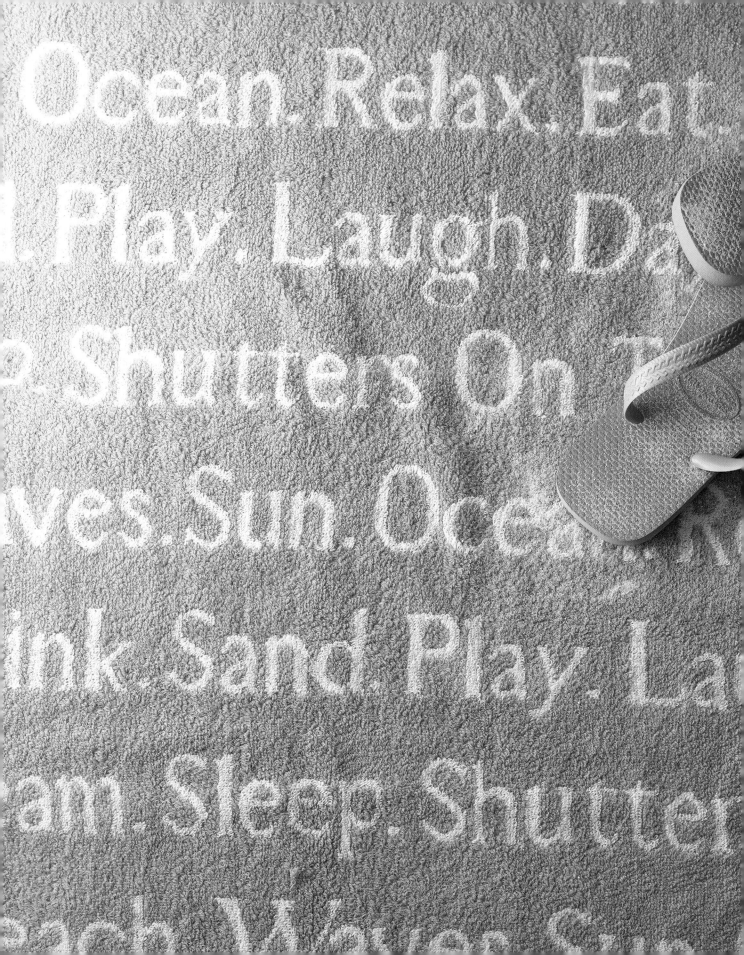

THE SUMMERTIME ANYTIME COOKBOOK

RECIPES FROM Shutters on the Beach

DANA SLATKIN

photographs by Amy Neunsinger

CLARKSON POTTER / PUBLISHERS

NEW YORK

All rights reserved. Published in the United States by Clarkson Potter/Publishers, an imprint of the Crown Publishing Group, a division of Random House, Inc., New York.

www.crownpublishing.com

www.clarksonpotter.com

Clarkson N. Potter is a trademark and Potter and colophon are registered trademarks of Random House, Inc.

Library of Congress Cataloging-in-Publication Data

Slatkin, Dana.

The summertime anytime cookbook: recipes from Shutters on the Beach / Dana Slatkin. — 1st ed.

1. Cookery, American — California style. 2. Shutters on the Beach (Santa Monica, Calif.) I. Title.

TX715.2.C34S57 2008   2007033205

641.59794 — dc22

978-0-307-38123-1

Printed in China

Design by Maureen Erbe, Rita Sowins/Erbe Design

10 9 8 7 6 5 4 3 2 1

First Edition

TO A, B, C, D, AND E
AND TO MOM

INTRODUCTION

I have lived with a beach in my backyard for nearly all of my life. And since it opened in 1993, my beach house—and family business—has been a posh little hotel in Santa Monica called Shutters on the Beach. Located front and center on one of the most popular beaches on the California coastline, our lovely urban refuge has been a continual source of inspiration for me, both inside and outside the kitchen.

All driftwood gray shingles and seaside charm, Shutters is where guests can be found lounging with a laptop on the pool deck, catching a well-earned nap in an elegant guest room, or sipping a nightcap by the fireplace in the cozy lobby. Shutters is also renowned for serving delightful farmers' market-fresh meals at its two restaurants, where the fare is breezy and unpretentious, served in a glorious setting with gracious hospitality.

Given the time my family and I have spent at the hotel over the years, I am constantly asked for recipes—the welcoming

Plum Tomato Soup with Baby Grilled Cheese Sandwiches that once greeted a delighted guest in her room, those impossibly fluffy Lemon-Ricotta Pancakes, the luscious warm Chocolate Pudding Cakes—or for secrets to decorating a bedroom with the warmth and style of room 302.

I set out to write this book in response to these and countless other requests from friends, family, and guests. But a few years and many meals later, I realized that our beach house also affirms much of what I believe to be meaningful and right in this world: gathering good company together for a meal; giving to those we love through simple, artful cooking; and bringing the beauty and freedom of the beach into our everyday lives. These are the simple pleasures we share at Shutters, and I hope this book will inspire you to make more time for them.

I have adapted some of my favorite recipes from Shutters' kitchens so they are relatively easy to prepare and enjoy at home. Like a day at the beach, these dishes don't require a lot of fuss or fancy equipment. Our cooking honors the bounty of the seasons with simple yet festive flair. Each recipe is an invitation to slow down, shed the need for domestic goddess perfection, and welcome good company into your home—no matter how far you may be from a real beach or what the weather has in store.

Here in Santa Monica, we are fortunate to be able to enjoy our beaches all year round. And yet, life at the beach revolves around the weather. With blue skies above, I like to quickly throw a meal together, gather the family and some friends, and get out to enjoy the day. When the weather is less cooperative, I'll invest a little more time in the kitchen, put on some jazz music, and linger at home with the kids.

So I have organized the recipes accordingly. There are carefree picnics and refreshing lunches for sunny days and uplifting meals for cloudy days. You'll find light, sexy dishes for balmy evenings and romantic comfort foods to share on stormy nights. There are also breakfast dishes worthy of an early rise, and basic sauces and vinaigrettes that will enliven your repertoire.

Though I have spent half of my life in various professional kitchens, from cooking school to three-star restaurants in France to the facilities that manufactured my retail line of snacks and baked goods, what stirs me most is the kind of low-key luxury that goes on at our hotel twenty-four hours a day, seven days a week. It is the way of life I aspire to even when we are not at the beach. It is a way of savoring each meal and each day with gusto, with a casual insouciance that makes us feel like it's summertime anytime.

With this book as your guide, I look forward to sharing with you some of our recipes and style secrets so you can bring home a taste of the beach. If you've ever been captivated by the ocean, relished the warm sand under your feet, or found solace in a salty breeze, you know the beach can rejuvenate your soul. These pages will hopefully put you in that delicious, life-affirming state of mind.

And make sure to gather plenty of good company around you, because life at the beach is best when shared!

—DANA SLATKIN

THE STORY OF
SHUTTERS ON THE BEACH

It all began in 1992, when two brothers purchased a half-completed beachfront hotel situated directly on the boardwalk of Santa Monica Beach. It was a sleepy enclave, mostly populated by surfers, old-timers from neighboring Venice Beach, and weekend devotees. The beach had a reputation for being tainted with pollution, and only the most intrepid would brave the icy waves for the occasional early-morning thrill.

But to the brothers, the location was a knockout, and they knew they had found a diamond in the rough. They had learned about hotels growing up at one of the most legendary, the Beverly Hills Hotel, which their family had owned and operated for thirty-five years. So with some inspiration from the beachside resorts that once dotted the Southern California coast in the 1920s and 1930s, the brothers began the renovation and completion of Shutters on the Beach.

From the beginning, their mission was to take the beach experience to a new level, to combine the simple, restorative pleasures of the beach with the elegance and comforts of a luxury hotel. They enlisted the help of a team of talented designers and hotel professionals to complete their vision. A year later, the hotel—named after the crisp white shutters that punctuate the guestrooms and shingled exteriors—opened to instantaneous success.

The broad stretch of Santa Monica Beach in front of Shutters has since been combed clean and invigorated with a pulsing vitality. Every day, throngs of beachgoers descend upon the wide sands, bike path, and pier to enjoy a delightful stint at the shore. With more than 340 days of sunshine each year, it is a dreamy backdrop for the ultimate urban beach retreat.

Inside Shutters' cozy lobby, with its dark hardwood floors and beamed ceilings, two fireplaces crackle year-round. The walls are adorned with contemporary art by renowned artists such as Richard Diebenkorn, Claus Oldenburg, and Jasper Johns. Other guests gather on the pool deck or a balcony to take in the sensational beach views. The two hundred guest rooms are sophisticated yet understated. There are no ornate flower arrangements, shocking colors, or gilded furniture to compete with the natural beauty of the surroundings. Shutters feels like a well-appointed home by the sea.

Over the years, the hotel has been the setting for countless marriage proposals, romantic retreats, picturesque weddings, power breakfasts, celebrity hobnobbing, and glittering parties. Along with its sister hotel next door, Casa Del Mar, Shutters remains one of the very few beachfront resorts on the California Coast and one of the most adored. But it is most known for its loving dedication to every detail of the memorable seaside experience. After all, at Shutters, life really is a day at the beach. . . .

SUNNYDAYS

Nothing says summer like a sunny day at the beach. And though a heavenly day of sunshine and warm sea breezes needs no embellishment, a delicious meal under a cloudless sky can't hurt.

When the day heats up, the biggest decision becomes whether to enjoy lunch outside or in and, of course, what to eat for dessert. The recipes in this chapter make the dilemma a little easier. Light and satisfying even on the most scorching day, recipes such as Cucumber Gazpacho, Grilled Chicken Club Sandwich, and Raspberry-Coconut Bars are a breeze to prepare, mix and match, and transport.

The only imperative of a sunny day is to savor each moment and each bite, for the one sure thing is that the weather, like our appetites, will be slightly different tomorrow.

SUNNYDAYS

Melon Agua Fresca

Strawberry Limeade

Pomegranate Mojito

Cucumber Gazpacho

Salad of Bocconcini, Cucumber, Tomato, and Olives

White Asparagus Salad with Blood Orange Vinaigrette

Shutters Chopped Salad

Seaside Slaw

Seared Tuna Salad Niçoise with Green Beans, Olives, and Sherry Vinaigrette

Pizza with Arugula, Plum Tomatoes, and Shaved Parmesan

Grilled Chicken Club Sandwich

Grilled Snapper Sandwich with Roasted Pepper Aïoli on Focaccia

Grilled Eggplant and Mozzarella Sandwich on Country Bread

Dungeness Crab Cakes with Avocado Tartar Sauce

Oven-Dried Tomato, Mozzarella, and Vegetable Skewers

Lemon-Ginger Cookies

Peanut-Butterscotch Crunch Bars

Chocolate-Caramel Brownies

Raspberry-Coconut Bars

Iced Nougat with Honey and Figs

MELON AGUA FRESCA

On a sweltering day, serve this traditional Mexican beverage over ice for an instant cool-down. Try using your favorite fruits, such as mango, pineapple, watermelon, honeydew, and peach in place of the melon. Frozen fruits will work just fine, too (defrost them first for a smoother consistency). For extra effervescence, use sparkling instead of flat water. You can even spike this refreshing beverage with a shot of your favorite liquor (try Midori melon liqueur, a fruit-flavored schnapps, or vodka).

2 cups roughly chopped cantaloupe
1 tablespoon fresh lemon or lime juice
¼ cup sugar, or more to taste
Lime or lemon wedges, for garnish

serves four

In a blender, combine 4 cups cold water with the cantaloupe and purée until smooth. Pour the mixture through a strainer into a pitcher or serving container. Add the lemon juice and sugar and stir until the sugar dissolves. Refrigerate for at least 2 hours or overnight. Serve in tall glasses (preferably chilled) with the lime or lemon wedges.

STRAWBERRY LIMEADE

One blistering day last summer, my kids decided they wanted to launch a lemonade stand. All we had in the house was a bag of limes and some frozen strawberries, so we flung them together in the blender and this drink was born. Not too sugary, not too tart, it's a simple way to taste summer all year 'round.

Juice of 12 limes, plus 1 lime, sliced, for garnish
1 (16-ounce) bag frozen strawberries
¾ cup sugar

serves six

Pour the lime juice into a blender. Add the strawberries and sugar and blend until smooth. Add 6 cups cold water and blend again until well mixed. Pour into glasses (preferably chilled) and garnish with the lime slices.

POMEGRANATE
MOJITO

This ruby red elixir was my drink of choice during all three of my pregnancies and is still my favorite virgin beverage — it's bubbly, thirst quenching, and full of those antioxidants that are so good for us. The combination of pomegranate, lime, and mint is stellar. You can find pomegranate syrup in many supermarkets, specialty stores, and online (see Source Guide). You might also try using pomegranate juice, which is not as concentrated in flavor but delicious as well.

6 sprigs fresh mint
1 lime, cut into 6 wedges
6 ounces pomegranate syrup (¾ cup)
Ice cubes
1 (1-liter) bottle sparkling water

serves six

Put a sprig of fresh mint and a lime wedge into each of 6 rocks glasses. Crush lightly with the back of a spoon or a muddler to release the flavors. Pour 1 ounce of pomegranate syrup into each glass, and then fill each glass with ice cubes and sparkling water. Stir and serve.

CUCUMBER GAZPACHO

This refreshing soup is the perfect preamble to a light, healthy meal. I love to serve it when entertaining by the pool or dining al fresco. It has a bit more verve than the ubiquitous tomato gazpacho, its lovely shade of light green complements any table or picnic basket, and it can conveniently be prepared in advance. For added flair, serve the soup in decorative salted glasses (simply rub the rims of the glasses with a wedge of lime, dip them into a plate of kosher salt, and chill before serving).

3 cups plain yogurt, preferably Greek-style or whole milk
5 medium English cucumbers, peeled, seeded, and roughly chopped
½ bunch celery (about 4 long stalks), roughly chopped
1 green bell pepper, seeded and roughly chopped
3 scallions, white and green parts, roughly chopped
½ bunch fresh cilantro, leaves and stems
½ bunch fresh dill, leaves only, plus a few sprigs for garnish
Kosher salt and freshly ground black pepper
Sugar
2 medium pink radishes, grated, for garnish

1. In a blender, purée the yogurt, cucumbers, celery, bell peppers, scallions, cilantro, and dill in batches until smooth. Season with salt, pepper, and sugar to taste. Cover and refrigerate for at least 2 hours or up to 2 days.

2. Serve the soup in chilled bowls or salted glasses with dill sprigs and grated radish for garnish.

POOL PERFECT

Lounging by the pool with the beach as your backdrop is the best of all worlds, and at Shutters, the combination is dreamy. But whether you have a pool, a beach, or simply a private spot with a patch of sun, you can elevate the day by integrating a little over-the-top hotel hospitality.

Refreshing beverages Set out icy pitchers of assorted drinks, such as a Melon Agua Fresca (page 18), water loaded with fresh berries or citrus slices, and Arnold Palmers, a favorite of us Angelenos (half iced tea, half freshly squeezed lemonade). To keep them ice cold, load them up with plastic ice cubes so they don't dilute in the heat.

Frozen fresh fruit Serve small bowls of chilled berries or frozen fruit skewers (make them the night before using fresh melon, grapes, mango, and pineapple chunks) over ice.

Lounging essentials To really coddle company, arrange baskets of sunscreen, magazines, crossword puzzle books, the latest page-turner novels, and the daily newspapers.

Towels Spray oversized towels with lavender water or lemon water (see Source Guide) to give them a fresh scent, roll them up, tie them with thick ribbon or twine, and garnish with a lavender sprig, rosebud, or new lip balm.

Mist bottles Provide guests with a breezy way to beat the heat by offering individual Evian atomizers or spray bottles filled with chilled water in a bucket of ice.

Chilled scented face towels For extra-steamy days, this invigorating indulgence will have your guests believing they are at a spa. Steep washcloths or thick paper hand towels in a brew of green or chamomile tea with a few drops of almond or coconut extract. Squeeze them out, roll them up, and chill them in the refrigerator or a cooler. Present them in a lovely b

SALAD of BOCCONCINI, CUCUMBER, TOMATO, AND OLIVES

Zesty and colorful, this salad features some of summer's best flavors. It is a lively riff on the ubiquitous Caprese salad, with cucumber, red onion, and black olives contributing added color, texture, and punch. Feel free to add other diced vegetables, such as avocado, hearts of palm, or cooked green beans.

1 medium English cucumber, diced
¼ small red onion, thinly sliced
½ cup pitted black olives, preferably niçoise or kalamata
Fresh Herb Vinaigrette (page 239)
Kosher salt and freshly ground black pepper
12 ounces fresh mozzarella bocconcini, halved if larger than bite-sized
3 medium plum or heirloom tomatoes, diced
Fresh basil leaves, thinly sliced, for garnish

In a medium bowl, combine the cucumber, onion, and olives. Toss the vegetables with the vinaigrette and season with salt and pepper. Add the bocconcini and tomatoes and toss gently. Divide among 4 serving plates and top each salad with some basil.

WHITE ASPARAGUS SALAD WITH BLOOD ORANGE VINAIGRETTE

serves four

Delicate, mild-mannered white asparagus makes a brief cameo appearance at farmers' markets and in grocers' produce sections each spring. Grab it when you spot it or you'll miss the opportunity to create this simple, sexy salad. The blood orange vinaigrette adds a tart-sweet flourish the color of a sunset. If blood oranges are not available, use tangerines or navel oranges. Also, keep in mind that unlike green asparagus, white asparagus should be cooked until it is quite tender, not al dente. Adding a little sugar and butter to the water during cooking keeps the asparagus from becoming bitter or tough.

2 tablespoons unsalted butter or extra-virgin olive oil
1 tablespoon sugar
Kosher salt
20 medium spears white asparagus, tough ends trimmed
6 blood oranges
1 tablespoon champagne vinegar
1 tablespoon honey
2 small shallots, minced
½ cup grapeseed oil
1 sprig fresh mint, leaves only

1. Bring a 5-quart pot of water to a boil with the butter, sugar, and 1 tablespoon salt. Have ready a medium bowl of ice water.

2. Using a vegetable peeler, peel each asparagus stalk beginning 3 inches from the tip, being careful to peel completely through the tough skin. Cut the bottom ½ inch off of each stalk. Cook the asparagus in the boiling water for about 8 to 9 minutes, until tender; carefully remove with a skimmer and plunge into the ice water to stop the cooking. Drain the asparagus and pat dry on a clean kitchen towel. The asparagus can be cooked up to 1 day in advance and kept refrigerated.

3. Peel the oranges with a paring knife, completely removing all of the white pith as you go. Remove each segment by slicing between the membranes, catching the juices in a small bowl. Squeeze any remaining juice into the bowl; you should have about ¼ cup. Add the vinegar, honey, and shallots. While stirring with a whisk, gradually add the oil; season with salt to taste. Reserve the orange segments in a separate bowl. The vinaigrette and orange segments can be kept refrigerated overnight.

4. To assemble the salad, arrange the asparagus on 4 serving plates. Carefully stir the orange segments into the vinaigrette and gently spoon over the asparagus. Sprinkle each salad with mint leaves.

SHUTTERS
CHOPPED SALAD

Everyone loves a chopped salad for its bite-sized mélange of goodies. What's more, it's easy to customize according to your own preferences. Toss in leftovers from this morning's breakfast or last night's dinner, such as bacon, hard-boiled eggs, chicken, grilled shrimp, or grilled tuna. The key is that everything is chopped into even bits.

3 hearts of romaine lettuce, chopped into small pieces

1 (14-ounce) can hearts of palm, drained and chopped

3 ripe yet firm tomatoes, seeded and chopped

1 (8-ounce) box white mushrooms, washed (see below) and chopped

3 stalks celery, chopped

1 small bunch chives, chopped

2 avocados

Juice of ½ lemon

Kosher salt and freshly ground black pepper

Louie Dressing (page 243)

1. In a large salad bowl, toss together the lettuce, hearts of palm, tomatoes, mushrooms, celery, and chives. Keep refrigerated until ready to serve, or for up to 2 hours.

2. Just before serving, halve and pit the avocados. Scoop out the flesh with a large spoon and dice the same size as the other ingredients. Sprinkle the pieces with the lemon juice and add to the salad bowl.

3. Season the salad with salt and pepper and toss lightly with the dressing. Divide among 8 chilled serving bowls or plates and serve.

How to Wash Mushrooms

Many types of mushrooms actually grow in trees, not in dirt, and are thus brought to market relatively clean. However, it is always best to give all mushrooms a good wash before using them, even if you buy them prewashed and sliced. Though most cooks will tell you to never wash mushrooms in water, or they will become soggy and lose their flavor, I have not found this to be true. In fact, I still use a little trick I learned in cooking school to wash all my mushrooms, and the mushrooms come out squeaky clean and grit-free. Fill a large bowl with cold water. Add a handful of flour and swish it around the water with your hand (the flour is both abrasive and bleaching). Dunk the whole mushrooms into the water and quickly swirl them around (leave the stems on, as they prevent the mushrooms from soaking up too much water). Immediately lift out the mushrooms and put them onto a clean dish towel to dry gently and thoroughly.

SEASIDE SLAW

With its crunch, punch, and garlicky kick, this lively coleslaw makes up for all the deficiencies of soggy deli versions. The fresh Napa cabbage and shredded carrots retain their texture for several days, making this an ideal side dish to transport for a picnic. Conveniently, the flavor improves the longer the slaw marinates in the light, tangy-sweet dressing.

⅓ cup Basic Aïoli (page 235) or mayonnaise
2 tablespoons cider vinegar
1 tablespoon sugar, or more to taste
1 teaspoon Dijon mustard
1 teaspoon fennel seeds
3 cups finely shredded Napa cabbage (1 small head)
1 large carrot, shredded
1 small red onion or 4 scallions, white and green parts, thinly sliced
Kosher salt and freshly ground black pepper

1. In a large bowl, whisk together the aïoli, vinegar, sugar, mustard, and fennel seeds.

2. Add the cabbage, carrot, and onion, seasoning with salt, pepper, and additional sugar if desired, and mix well. The coleslaw may be made 3 days ahead and refrigerated in an airtight container.

FAVORITE SUNNY-DAY
BEACH ACTIVITIES

When the sun is blazing, my first instinct is to pack up the car and head straight for the beach. Between the ocean, bike path, sand, and pier, there are a hundred different ways to frolic in Santa Monica, but my family always prefers these tried-and-true favorites:

Cruise Along the Beach Lucky for us locals, the Santa Monica bike trail is right outside our door. The longest beach path of its kind in the world, it stretches 22 miles from Malibu to Venice Beach to Redondo Beach. This magnificent bike path is one of the most popular free public athletic amenities in all of California. It is our favorite way to sample Southern California beach culture at its best. Regardless of what kind of path you have access to, take advantage by navigating it on foot, roller skates, bicycle, or any nonmotorized vehicle available to you.

Play with Sand Those countless grains of sand are perfect for drawing, building, and creating. Try designing a dartboard in the sand and tossing rocks or shells to see who can get a bull's eye, or draw a tic-tac-toe square or a hopscotch court.

Hunt for Treasures Make up a list of things you can find on a beach—shells, rocks, seaweed, sand crabs, starfish, sand dollars—and start a race to find everything on the list. Collect your foraged finds in pails and bring them home to make souvenir collages or to use as table decorations.

Organize Relay Races on the Sand They are as much fun to watch as they are to participate in! Have children hold a beach ball between their legs and walk across the sand to deposit it into a large pail. Or bring some large sponges and have kids fill pails using their sponges by running back and forth from the ocean.

Make Tracks While Clearing Trash Bring a disposable shopping bag with you when you walk barefoot along the shore. Help clean up the beach at the same time by picking up trash along the way.

SEARED TUNA SALAD NIÇOISE WITH GREEN BEANS, OLIVES, AND SHERRY VINAIGRETTE

serves four

Practically every eatery within biking distance of a beach has imported this classic French salad. But here you'll find a few refined twists, like quail eggs and anchovy-stuffed green olives, which are worth the trouble to find but are not crucial to the success of the recipe. If you cannot find good-quality fresh tuna, use canned tuna packed in oil and drain it well. You can prepare and refrigerate each ingredient a day or two ahead and arrange them in large serving bowls or on a platter at the last minute.

8 ounces green beans, ends trimmed
1 pound fingerling or other small potatoes, halved if larger than bite-sized
8 quail eggs (see Source Guide), or 4 large hard-boiled eggs sliced in halves or quarters
1 tablespoon extra-virgin olive oil or grapeseed oil
12 ounces sushi-quality tuna (loin pieces if available) or 1 (12-ounce) can solid tuna packed in oil
Kosher salt and freshly ground black pepper
2 teaspoons Dijon mustard
2 hearts of romaine lettuce, leaves separated, torn into bite-sized pieces
2 tomatoes, cut into wedges
½ (8-ounce) can anchovy-stuffed green olives (see Source Guide), drained
2 tablespoons capers, drained
Sherry Vinaigrette (page 241)

1. Bring a large pot of salted water to a boil. Have ready a medium bowl of ice water. Cook the green beans until tender but still crisp, 6 to 8 minutes. With a skimmer, remove the beans and plunge them into the ice water to stop the cooking. Drain well in a colander and dry on a kitchen towel.

2. Add the potatoes to the boiling water and cook until the potatoes are tender when pierced with a knife, about 15 minutes. Remove with a skimmer and set aside; slice when cool.

3. Add the quail eggs to the boiling water and cook for about 5 minutes, or until hard boiled. Drain, cool under cold running water, peel, and halve; set aside.

4. In a small sauté pan, heat the oil over high heat until almost smoking. Meanwhile, season the tuna generously with salt and pepper on all sides. Sear the tuna, turning as needed, until it is just colored on all sides but still rare inside, 2 to 3 minutes. Transfer the tuna to a cutting board and let cool slightly. Brush the tuna with the mustard and then slice about ¼ inch thick.

5. In a large bowl, toss the lettuce, tomatoes, olives, capers, potatoes, and green beans with the Sherry Vinaigrette. Arrange on serving plates and top with the eggs and slices of tuna. Serve immediately.

PIZZA WITH ARUGULA, PLUM TOMATOES, AND SHAVED PARMESAN

makes 1 (12-inch) pizza, plus dough for another pizza;
serves 4 as a first course

A colorful presentation of pizza and salad in one, this dish sports a crust that is simultaneously crisp and puffy, with an unconventional mix of arugula, fresh tomatoes, basil, and shaved Parmesan cheese on top. The dough is easy to prepare by hand and can be left on its own for most of the day while you are going and doing. You will need a pizza stone and a baker's peel (paddle) to pull this off like a pro. If you prefer, substitute store-bought refrigerated dough (you'll need about 16 ounces for one large crust or two small ones). Save the slicing to the last minute so your guests can admire your creation!

PIZZA DOUGH
1 package (2 teaspoons) active dry yeast
1 tablespoon honey
3 tablespoons extra-virgin olive oil
½ tablespoon kosher salt
3¼ cups all-purpose flour
Cornmeal, for dusting

PIZZA
1 cup shredded mozzarella cheese
2 handfuls of arugula leaves
2 plum tomatoes, seeds removed, sliced
1 tablespoon chopped garlic
½ cup chopped fresh basil
2 tablespoons extra-virgin olive oil
1½ ounces Parmesan cheese, shaved
Kosher salt

1. Make the pizza dough: In a large bowl, combine the yeast, honey, and ¼ cup lukewarm water, stirring with a wooden spoon until the yeast has dissolved. Let stand for 5 minutes.

2. Stir in 1 tablespoon of the olive oil along with the salt, then add 1 cup of the flour and mix thoroughly using the wooden spoon. Gradually add ¾ cup more lukewarm water and the remaining 2¼ cups flour, alternating in small amounts and stirring well until the dough comes together and is soft but not sticky (you

recipe continues

might end up with a little water or flour left over). Turn the dough onto a lightly floured surface and knead well, about 10 minutes. Coat the inside of the bowl with another tablespoon of the oil, and then form the dough into a ball, put it into the bowl, turn the dough to coat it lightly with oil, and cover with plastic wrap. Set it aside to rise in a warm corner of the kitchen until it has doubled in volume, at least 3 hours or up to 6 hours.

3. At least 30 minutes before you are ready to bake, preheat the oven to 450°F. If you have a pizza stone, place it in the oven.

4. Sprinkle a baker's peel with cornmeal (or sprinkle a baking sheet with cornmeal). Divide the dough in half and wrap one in plastic wrap to save for a later use (the dough will keep refrigerated for 1 week or frozen for 2 months). Stretch and flatten the other dough half until it is very thin, forming a 12-inch circle, and place it on the peel (or baking sheet). Brush the dough lightly with the remaining 1 tablespoon oil and sprinkle with the mozzarella. With a jerk of the wrist, transfer the pizza to the pizza stone in the oven (or simply put the baking sheet in the oven) and bake until the crust is crisp on the bottom and the cheese is bubbling, about 20 minutes.

5. Meanwhile, in a small bowl, combine the arugula, tomatoes, garlic, basil, and olive oil. Remove the pizza from the oven, top with the arugula-and-tomato mixture, and sprinkle with the shaved Parmesan. Season with salt and slice into 8 pieces. Serve immediately.

GRILLED CHICKEN CLUB SANDWICH

makes 4 sandwiches

Just about every decent hotel menu offers some version of a chicken club. Three good reasons: It is the perfect comfort food, it combines all four food groups in one tidy stack, and it is just plain delicious. This recipe is for a traditional double-decker, though you can easily omit the extra bread if you are counting calories. You can also skip the bacon and cook the chicken in olive oil instead.

16 slices lean bacon
2 skinless and boneless chicken breast halves (about 1½ pounds)
Kosher salt and freshly ground black pepper
12 slices sourdough or whole-grain bread, lightly toasted
¼ cup mayonnaise or Basic Aïoli (page 235)
8 lettuce leaves
16 thin slices avocado
16 thin slices tomato
16 thin slices red onion

1. In a small heavy skillet, cook the bacon over medium heat, turning as needed, until it is crisp. Transfer the bacon to paper towels to drain; pour off all but 1 tablespoon of fat from the skillet.

2. Season the chicken breast halves liberally with salt and pepper. Add to the pan with the bacon fat and cook over medium heat for 6 to 8 minutes on each side, or until they are cooked through. Transfer them to a cutting board and let rest for 10 minutes, then slice thinly.

3. Spread one side of each slice of toast with a little mayonnaise and sprinkle with pepper to taste. Build the sandwiches starting with the toast, then adding 2 slices each of lettuce, avocado, tomato, onion, and then bacon. Top with a few slices of chicken. Cover each sandwich with another slice of toast and repeat the process. Finally, top each sandwich with the remaining toast, press down firmly, and secure each sandwich with toothpicks. Slice each sandwich diagonally and serve.

GRILLED SNAPPER SANDWICH WITH ROASTED PEPPER AÏOLI ON FOCACCIA

makes 4 sandwiches

Thick and flavorful, focaccia bread makes a perfect sandwich package, keeping what's inside fresh and crisp without becoming soggy. Any firm-fleshed fish will work well in this sandwich (try halibut, tuna, or swordfish). For a vegetarian alternative, substitute smoked tofu and cheese, or satisfy meat-lovers with roast beef or smoked turkey. In any case, it's hard to go wrong between two slices of focaccia!

Grapeseed or canola oil
4 (6-ounce) fillets red snapper, no more than ½ inch thick, skinless
Kosher salt and freshly ground black pepper
4 slices focaccia or other buns, halved crosswise
¼ cup Roasted Pepper Aïoli (page 237)
Bibb lettuce leaves
4 thin slices red onion
2 plum tomatoes, sliced
Pickle slices, sour or sweet, optional

1. Preheat a grill to high or heat a sauté pan over high heat. Lightly oil the grill or pour a thin film of oil into the pan to coat the bottom.

2. Season the fish with salt and pepper. Cook until both sides are nicely marked and the fish is cooked through, 3 to 4 minutes per side depending on thickness (the fish should flake easily and the internal temperature should be 145°F). Transfer the cooked fish to a plate.

3. Toast the sliced focaccia halves briefly on the grill or in a toaster oven. Spread them generously with aïoli, then stack the fish, lettuce, onion, tomato, and pickle on the bottom halves. Top with the other halves of focaccia. Serve the sandwiches with extra aïoli on the side.

BEACH
BLANKET CHIC

For a stylish moveable feast, consider adding some unexpected items to your picnic packing list.

A pretty cloth
Top your picnic blanket with a lovely tablecloth or piece of fabric. The bottom blanket will act as a barrier against sand and bugs while the cloth dresses it up any way you like.

Posh pillows
Bring a few cotton- or linen-covered cushions from around the house to create the coziness of an outdoor living room.

Groovy linens
You're going to end up washing the blanket and beach towels, so it's no extra trouble to add some cotton napkins to the mix. You'll cut down on the postpicnic trash, too.

Nifty buckets and pails
Instead of a cooler, bring a galvanized metal bucket packed with all of your staples, including a well-sealed bag of ice. Once you unload, fill the bucket with ice and bottled drinks. Bring smaller metal pails, and instead of serving food on plates, pack each pail with a little sandwich, salad, and dessert. Label each one so your guests can then use them to collect beach treasures after the meal.

A bouquet or pot of basil
This lovely centerpiece will keep yellow jackets away and add a verdant touch to your spread.

GRILLED EGGPLANT
AND MOZZARELLA SANDWICH
ON COUNTRY BREAD

makes 4 open-faced sandwiches

Substantial enough to satisfy even the most ardent carnivore, this open-faced sandwich makes a delightful picnic lunch or dinner. It also travels easily with an extra slice of bread and toothpicks. On a warm day, it is especially satisfying alongside a cold soup such as Cucumber Gazpacho (page 21), while on a brisk afternoon, I love to dip it in a big bowl of Plum Tomato Soup (page 58). Here, it's all about the bread—the crustier, the better!

1 large eggplant, sliced $\frac{1}{2}$ inch thick (16 slices)
8 tablespoons extra-virgin olive oil
Kosher salt and freshly ground black pepper
8 ounces mozzarella cheese, cut into 8 $\frac{1}{4}$-inch-thick slices
4 thick slices country bread
$\frac{1}{4}$ cup Roasted Pepper Aïoli (page 237) or Avocado Tartar Sauce (page 237)
$1\frac{1}{2}$ tablespoons balsamic vinegar
1 garlic clove, minced
4 large handfuls of arugula leaves
2 large tomatoes, chopped
3 tablespoons chopped fresh basil
2 tablespoons pine nuts, toasted (see page 126)

1. Preheat a grill to high or heat a sauté pan over high heat.

2. Brush the eggplant slices on both sides with 6 tablespoons of the olive oil and sprinkle them liberally with salt and pepper. Grill them until tender, turning occasionally, about 10 minutes.

3. Place 1 cheese slice atop each of 8 of the eggplant slices; top with the remaining eggplant slices. Grill until the cheese melts, about 2 minutes, and set aside on a plate.

4. Grill the bread slices briefly, until they are lightly marked, a minute or two. Transfer the grilled bread to serving plates, spread with Roasted Pepper Aïoli or Avocado Tartar Sauce, and top with 2 stacks of grilled eggplant and cheese.

5. Whisk the remaining 2 tablespoons oil with the vinegar and garlic in a medium bowl. Season the dressing with salt and pepper. Add the arugula, tomatoes, and basil; toss the salad and sprinkle with the pine nuts. Serve the salad alongside the sandwiches.

DUNGENESS CRAB CAKES
WITH AVOCADO TARTAR SAUCE

There are crab cake connoisseurs who judge a restaurant by its crab cakes. Many people say Shutters serves up some of the best crab cakes in town. It could be due to the buttery challah bread crumbs, or the traditional Old Bay seasoning, or the high crab-to-binder ratio. In any case, here is the recipe. I recommend serving them with Avocado Tartar Sauce and Roasted Pepper and Corn Succotash (page 136), but a small salad and Caper Rémoulade (page 238) or Roasted Pepper Aïoli (page 237) would be excellent partners, too. You could even make baby cakes (about a tablespoon each) and serve them as finger food at cocktail time.

1 pound lump crabmeat
¼ cup mayonnaise
1 large egg
2 tablespoons dried bread crumbs (preferably challah or brioche)
1 tablespoon Old Bay seasoning
⅛ teaspoon cayenne pepper, or to taste
¼ cup all-purpose flour
¼ cup extra-virgin olive oil or vegetable oil
Avocado Tartar Sauce (page 237)
Roasted Pepper and Corn Succotash (page 136; optional)

1. In a medium bowl, pick carefully through the crabmeat and remove any pieces of shell. Add the mayonnaise, egg, bread crumbs, and Old Bay and mix gently until the mixture just holds together. Season with cayenne pepper. Form into 6 cakes, each about ½ inch thick, and dust lightly on all sides with flour.

2. In a large skillet, preferably nonstick, heat the oil until very hot but not smoking. Add the crab cakes and cook until lightly browned, 4 to 5 minutes per side. Transfer to paper towels to absorb excess oil.

3. Serve the warm crab cakes on a platter with the Avocado Tartar Sauce and Roasted Pepper and Corn Succotash on the side.

recipe continues

NOTES

To make fish cakes, substitute 1 ½ pounds of chopped cooked fish for the crab. (I recommend steamed or poached cod, tilapia, or whitefish.) Add more bread crumbs if necessary to bind the mixture.

For vegetarian cakes, substitute 1 ½ pounds firm tofu that has been drained, pressed between paper towels (place a heavy object such as a pot on top of a paper towel on the block of tofu for about 15 minutes to help eliminate moisture), and diced. Lightly crumble the tofu while mixing and add more bread crumbs if necessary to bind the mixture.

Crab (or fish) cakes can be frozen raw (before dusting with flour) in an airtight container. You do not need to thaw them before dusting with flour and cooking them, though they may need a few extra minutes in the pan to heat all the way through.

OVEN-DRIED TOMATO, MOZZARELLA, AND VEGETABLE SKEWERS

makes 4 skewers; serves 2 to 4

Perfect as a light snack, first course, picnic nibble, or side dish for grilled main courses, these skewers are as colorful as they are flavorful. To dress them up on the spot, I use nifty flavored wood skewers (try citrus rosemary and garlic herb) that I discovered at a local gourmet shop.

4 (10-inch) bamboo skewers
¼ cup extra-virgin olive oil
Juice of 1 lemon
¼ teaspoon crushed red pepper flakes
1 garlic clove, minced
Kosher salt and freshly ground black pepper
1 medium zucchini, sliced
2 large portabello mushrooms, washed (see page 26), stemmed, and sliced in wedges
8 ounces fresh mozzarella cheese, cut into 1-inch cubes
16 pieces Oven-Dried Tomatoes (page 244)

1. Preheat a grill to high or heat a grill pan over high heat. Soak the skewers in cold water for 10 minutes to prevent them from burning on the grill. Drain and dry well.

2. In a small bowl, whisk together the oil, lemon juice, red pepper, and garlic; season generously with salt and pepper. Set aside.

3. Thread each skewer with the sliced zucchini and mushroom wedges. Drizzle with the dressing.

4. Grill the skewers, turning onto all sides, until the vegetables are tender, about 10 minutes.

5. Meanwhile, place a cube of mozzarella between 2 pieces of tomato and repeat until all the tomatoes are used.

6. Remove the skewers from the heat, add a tomato-wrapped mozzarella cube to each end, and return to the grill for 2 more minutes to rewarm. Serve immediately on a platter.

LEMON-GINGER COOKIES

makes about 2 dozen cookies

With the delicate charm of little sand dollars and a kiss of ginger, these subtly flavored cookies beg to be packed in your picnic basket or served alongside bowls of tropical sorbet. I like to make them on the crunchy side, but if you prefer your cookies chewy, reduce the baking time by 3 minutes.

½ cup (1 stick) unsalted butter
1 cup packed golden brown sugar
1 large egg
¼ cup sour cream
1 teaspoon lemon extract
1 teaspoon vanilla extract
1 teaspoon grated lemon zest
1¾ cups all-purpose flour
1 teaspoon baking soda
1 teaspoon cream of tartar
½ teaspoon kosher salt
1 teaspoon ground ginger
3 tablespoons minced candied ginger

1. Preheat the oven to 350°F. Lightly grease 2 baking sheets.

2. In a food processor or electric mixer, beat together the butter and brown sugar until light in color. Add the egg, sour cream, lemon and vanilla extracts, and lemon zest and beat until light and fluffy.

3. In a large bowl, sift together the flour, baking soda, cream of tartar, salt, and ground ginger. Add the butter mixture along with the candied ginger, and mix until blended thoroughly.

4. With floured or moistened fingers, drop by tablespoonfuls about 2 inches apart onto the prepared baking sheets. Shape the cookies into balls and flatten them down slightly with the palm of your hand.

5. Bake for 12 to 15 minutes, or until the cookies are set and lightly colored. If you wish, carve sand dollar–like slits into the cookies with the tip of a knife before they cool. Cool on a wire rack. The cookies will keep for up to 3 days in an airtight container.

PEANUT-BUTTERSCOTCH CRUNCH BARS

makes 16 bars

If you thought Rice Krispies treats were the last word in grab-and-go dessert bars, wait until you taste this exceptional no-bake confection of Special K cereal, chocolate, peanut butter, and butterscotch. These bars can be stored in an airtight container for up to 1 week, provided you can resist them.

½ cup sugar
1 cup light corn syrup
1 cup smooth, salted peanut butter
6 cups Special K cereal, crushed
1 cup milk chocolate or semisweet chocolate chips
1 cup butterscotch chips

1. Lightly grease a 9 × 12-inch glass baking dish.

2. In a large saucepan over low heat, dissolve the sugar into the corn syrup, being careful not to let the mixture boil.

3. Dissolve the peanut butter into the sugar mixture, turn off the flame, add the crushed cereal, and mix well.

4. Spread the cereal mixture evenly into the prepared baking dish.

5. Over a double boiler or in a microwave, melt the chocolate and butterscotch chips together. Spread the topping over the cereal mixture and let it stand at room temperature until firm, about 1 hour. Cut into 2 × 3-inch bars.

CHOCOLATE-CARAMEL
BROWNIES

makes 20 brownies

When it comes to a brownie, there's no such thing as one that's too chocolatey or too gooey. This recipe is for everyone who agrees. It is shamelessly sweet already, so use bittersweet chocolate for the best results. If you tightly wrap and refrigerate the extra Caramel Sauce, you can reach for it again when serving Classic Chocolate Pudding Cakes (page 197), Warm Pineapple Upside-Down Cake (page 194), Peach-Blackberry Crumble (page 96), or simply a bowl of your favorite ice cream. (See photograph, page 46.)

1 cup (2 sticks) unsalted butter,
   plus more for baking dish
16 ounces bittersweet chocolate, chopped
4 large eggs
2 cups sugar
1 teaspoon vanilla extract

1 1/2 cups all-purpose flour
1/2 teaspoon kosher salt
3/4 cup Caramel Sauce (page 249)
Confectioners' sugar, for dusting, optional

1. Preheat the oven to 325°F. Butter a 9 × 12-inch glass baking dish and line it with overlapping strips of wax paper to prevent the brownies from sticking.

2. Bring 2 inches of water to a simmer in a medium pot. Put the butter and 12 ounces of the chocolate in a large sauté pan and set the pan over the pot of simmering water, stirring occasionally, until melted. Set aside to cool.

3. In a large metal bowl, whisk the eggs and sugar over the same pot of simmering water until they are warm and the sugar has dissolved. Remove the bowl from the heat and continue whisking until the mixture is light in color, about 3 minutes. Add the vanilla and the cooled chocolate mixture.

4. In a separate bowl, sift together the flour and salt, then fold them into the batter.

5. Pour half of the batter into the prepared baking dish and bake until just set, 10 to 12 minutes. Remove the brownies from the oven and sprinkle them with the remaining 4 ounces chocolate. Drizzle the Caramel Sauce on top and drop the remaining batter over the caramel, spreading it evenly. Return the dish to the oven to bake for another 15 to 20 minutes, until the batter is set and cracks appear on the surface (the brownies should be a bit gooey inside).

6. Cool the brownies in the baking dish, then carefully invert them onto another sheet of wax paper and peel away the wax paper used in baking. Dust them with confectioners' sugar and cut into rectangles. The brownies will keep in an airtight container for up to 3 days.

RASPBERRY-COCONUT BARS

makes 16 bars

A fruity twist on the ubiquitous lemon bar, this recipe is a breezy way to finish a picnic or a light sunny-day meal. Because the topping is quite sweet, use a tangy, low-sugar jam for the filling. Apricot and blueberry jams also work beautifully with the bars' golden coconut crust. (See photograph, page 46.)

CRUST AND FILLING

1 cup all-purpose flour

1 teaspoon baking powder

½ cup (1 stick) unsalted butter or margarine, softened

1 large egg, beaten

1 teaspoon milk

1 cup raspberry jam, preferably a low-sugar version (see Source Guide)

TOPPING

1 cup sugar

1 teaspoon vanilla extract

1½ cups sweetened flaked coconut

3 tablespoons unsalted butter, softened

1 large egg, beaten

1. Preheat the oven to 350°F.

2. Prepare the crust in a medium bowl: Mix together the flour, baking powder, butter, egg, and milk using your fingers or a wooden spoon. Press into the bottom of an 8 × 8-inch or 11 × 7-inch baking pan or glass baking dish, allowing the dough to climb up the sides a bit. Spread the jam evenly over the dough.

3. Make the topping in the same bowl: Combine the sugar, vanilla, coconut, butter, and egg and blend with your fingers (don't worry if it is sticky). Drop the topping evenly over the jam filling.

4. Bake for about 30 minutes, or until the topping is lightly golden. Cool completely before cutting into squares. The bars will keep in an airtight container for up to 2 days.

ICED NOUGAT WITH HONEY AND FIGS

serves six

This lighthearted frozen dessert is the perfect antidote to dessert ennui. Crunchy candied almonds are mixed into a chilled soufflé mixture along with shaved chocolate, then frozen and topped with port-soaked figs. It's a feather-light take on cookies 'n' cream ice cream, with an unexpected crunch and a luscious drunken fig topping.

¼ cup plus 2 tablespoons sugar
⅓ cup slivered almonds, toasted (see page 126)
3 tablespoons honey
2 tablespoons light corn syrup
3 large egg whites
⅔ cup heavy cream
1 ounce bittersweet chocolate, shaved with a vegetable peeler
12 ripe figs, quartered (see Note)
¼ cup red port wine

1. Grease a baking sheet and set aside.

2. In a small saucepan, combine ¼ cup of the sugar and 2 tablespoons water; bring to a simmer over medium heat. Cook until the water evaporates and the mixture turns a golden caramel color. Remove the pan from the heat and stir in the almonds. Turn the mixture out onto the prepared baking sheet and let it cool completely. Use a spoon or rolling pin to crush it into small pieces.

3. Bring 2 inches of water to a simmer in a medium pot. Prepare the meringue: In an electric mixer bowl, combine the honey, remaining 2 tablespoons sugar, corn syrup, and egg whites. Place the bowl over the simmering water and whisk the egg white mixture slowly until all of the sugar has dissolved. Return the bowl to the mixer and whip the meringue on high speed until it is fluffy and cool to the touch.

4. In a large bowl, whip the cream to stiff peaks using a whisk. Fold the meringue, chocolate shavings, and almond nougat into the cream. Ladle the mixture into 6 glasses or ramekins; freeze for at least 2 hours.

5. An hour before serving, marinate the figs in the port. To serve, spoon the figs and juices into the glasses.

NOTE
If you miss the brief fresh fig season (August through September), use dried figs instead. Put the dried figs and port in a small saucepan and simmer over low heat for about 10 minutes. The figs will become soft, and the sugary juices become a delicious sauce. Let cool before serving.

STOCKING YOUR KITCHEN

Fortunately, the fresh, lively flavors of beach cooking do not require fancy equipment or daily jaunts to a gourmet grocer, but they do begin with quality ingredients. With a few strategic shopping trips, you can pull together a fantastic meal quickly so you can get out and enjoy the day.

If you're lucky enough to live or vacation near a good local farmers' market, take advantage. There you will find dedicated growers offering the best of their crops, a menagerie that might include sweet corn and ripe tomatoes in summer and a rainbow of squashes, apples, and pears in fall. Though some of the produce may not look as perfect as the waxed and sprayed supermarket versions, their flavor and texture will almost always make up for any surface imperfections. I also rest easier knowing that minimal environmental pollutants (such as fossil fuels and pesticides) have been used to produce my food. There is no question that buying organic is simply better for our bodies, oceans, and planet.

But before you forage for fresh goods, I recommend stocking up on some essentials. Unless otherwise noted, the following items can be kept in a cool dry place at room temperature for up to one year.

Oils Olive, canola, and grapeseed are my top three. Extra-virgin olive oil is my favorite for vinaigrettes, mayonnaise, and sauces cooked over low or medium heat; it is the only type of olive oil called for in this book's recipes. Look for one with a light green color, indicating that it is both flavorful and high in antioxidants. For baking and frying, I use canola oil. It is lighter in color and texture than many other oils and neutral in flavor. I use grapeseed oil for sautéing and searing foods at high heat. It doesn't burn as quickly as other oils and is one of the heart-healthiest oils available. If temperatures in your home regularly get above 80°F, consider storing oils in the refrigerator to prevent spoilage or buying them in small quantities.

Vinegars Stocking only one type of vinegar is like keeping only one beverage in the house. I always like to have a few options on hand, including white wine, red wine, sherry, champagne, and rice vinegars. Though the recipes in this book may recommend a specific one to use, feel free to experiment and decide on your favorite pairings.

Broths Making a rich, aromatic stock from scratch is a fantasy for most of us, so I don't think twice about buying one from the supermarket. Look for chicken, beef, and vegetable broths sold in a box (so that they do not taste like a tin can), that are low in sodium (better to add your own seasoning to taste), and that contain no preservatives or additives such as MSG. Once opened, broths should be refrigerated and used within one week.

Dried mushrooms Keep dried morels, porcinis, or shiitakes around for enhancing soups and adding depth to sauces. Rehydrate them with just enough boiling water to cover them, then strain and save the soaking liquid to use in place of broth.

Herbs, spices, and seasonings Start with kosher salt; its larger grains lessen the likelihood of accidental oversalting and create a nonstick barrier when applied to fish or meat before cooking. Also make sure you have whole peppercorns (I buy a premixed blend of black, white, pink and green; see Source Guide) and a good peppermill; the taste of freshly ground pepper is dramatically better than preground selections. Additional requisites include dried thyme, basil, oregano (leaf, not ground); whole fennel, coriander, and cumin seeds; ground cinnamon and nutmeg; and vanilla extract.

Canned or frozen vegetables and beans Sometimes frozen produce is even tastier than the fresh alternative, depending on the time of year. Peas, corn, and spinach are all good options to keep on hand in the freezer. I also keep cans of chickpeas, cannellini beans, hearts of palm, and different varieties of pitted olives to toss in salads, soups, or pasta sauces.

Unsalted butter How many times have you reached for a stick of butter only to realize you're out? I keep a couple pounds in the freezer for whenever it's needed, and I always cook with unsalted butter to better control seasoning.

Premium chocolate Keep bittersweet and semisweet chocolate around in bricks and chips for baking (and snacking). As for milk and white chocolate, buy them only when a recipe calls for them; they get stale quicker and can absorb aromas of spices that are next to them. Always store chocolate in airtight bags or containers in a cool dry place.

CLOUDYDAYS

Some days at the shore are as moody as we are. The soft gray blanket of morning fog may not lift all day, or it may fade ever so gradually, revealing a patchwork of sun-speckled sky. These are the days when I am most inspired to bundle up, burrow, and cook.

At Shutters, there is a meal for any mood. When sun is out of the question, the comfort foods in this chapter seem to best fit the bill. For maximum conviviality, serve them family-style—Sweet Corn Chowder with Cumin and Cilantro served right from the pot or a heady platter of Strozzapreti with Sausage, White Beans, Broccolini, and Oven-Dried Tomatoes is sure to be a crowd-pleaser. Add a couple wholesome sides like Buttermilk Onion Rings or Tuscan Kale, and end with a sweetly reassuring dessert such as Malted Chocolate Cream Pie, and spirits will be warm and bright even if the day is not.

CLOUDYDAYS

Plum Tomato Soup with Baby Grilled Cheese Sandwiches

Tomatillo, Chile, and Bean Chowder

Sweet Corn Chowder with Cumin and Cilantro

Citrus-Cured Tuna with Pickled Carrot and Radish Salad

Harvest Salad of Apples, Pecans, and Goat Cheese with Apple Vinaigrette

Caesar Salad with Parmesan Crisps

Wild Mushroom Salad with Two Dressings

Toasted Pearl Pasta with Rock Shrimp, Green Beans, and Garlic

Strozzapreti with Sausage, White Beans, Broccolini, and Oven-Dried Tomatoes

Shutters Vegetarian Burger

Seared Sea Bass with Black Bean Sauce

Roasted Halibut with Tomato-Juniper Compote

Roasted Salmon with Grain Mustard and Herbs

Roasted Chicken Breasts with Creamy Grits

Mexican Pot Roast

Roasted Rack of Lamb with Sun-Dried Cherry Sauce

Lemon-Ginger String Beans

Savoy Cabbage and Spinach

Tuscan Kale

Buttermilk Onion Rings

Apple-Cinnamon Crisp

Lemon Tart

Peach-Blackberry Crumble

Malted Chocolate Cream Pie

Strawberry Shortcake

Berries with Chocolate-Coconut Fondue

PLUM TOMATO SOUP
WITH BABY GRILLED CHEESE
SANDWICHES

serves four

Tap into your inner child with this classic comfort food duo. Warm and reassuring, the soup is as pure and flavorful as a tomato soup should be. For a slightly richer feel, add a cup of cream in the last 5 minutes of cooking. For the sandwiches, choose your favorite cheese (we are crazy for chive-packed Cotswold Cheddar, available at cheese shops and gourmet markets) to make this dish anything but routine. (See photograph, page 57.)

SOUP

2 tablespoons extra-virgin olive oil
½ yellow onion, chopped
4 garlic cloves, minced
1 medium stalk celery, chopped
1 medium carrot, chopped
2 sprigs fresh basil or 1 teaspoon dried
1 sprig fresh oregano or ½ teaspoon dried
1 (28-ounce) can Italian whole plum tomatoes with juice
2 cups low-sodium chicken or vegetable broth
Kosher salt and freshly ground black pepper
Sugar

SANDWICHES

8 ounces sharp Cheddar cheese, cut into 8 slices
8 slices good crusty bread
Salted butter, softened

1. Prepare the soup: In a medium pot, heat the olive oil over medium-low heat and add the onion, garlic, celery, and carrot. Cover and cook until tender, about 5 minutes. Add the basil, oregano, and tomatoes and simmer uncovered for 10 minutes. Add the broth, bring to a boil, then lower the heat and simmer for another 10 to 15 minutes. Remove from the heat and allow to cool for a few minutes.

2. In a blender, purée the soup carefully in batches. Pass it through a sieve back into the pot. Adjust the seasoning with salt, pepper, and sugar; keep warm over low heat while you prepare the sandwiches. (Alternatively, the soup can be cooled, covered, and refrigerated for 2 days or frozen for up to 1 month.)

3. Prepare the sandwiches: Place 2 slices of cheese in between 2 slices of bread for each sandwich. Spread butter on the outer sides of the 4 sandwiches. In a medium sauté pan over medium heat, brown the sandwiches lightly on both sides until the bread is crispy and the cheese is soft and melted, using a small pan placed on top of the sandwiches as a weight (alternatively, use a sandwich press). Cut the sandwiches diagonally into small triangles.

4. Pour the soup into bowls and serve the sandwiches on the side.

TOMATILLO, CHILE, AND BEAN CHOWDER

When you are in the mood for a nourishing, chunky, and unusual soup, try this hearty Mexican-inspired chowder. Full of complexity with a subtle dash of heat, it strikes a happy medium between spicy and mild.

2 tablespoons extra-virgin olive oil
1 pound yellow onions, diced
3 medium fresh poblano chiles, seeded and cut into thin strips
1 tablespoon finely slivered garlic
2 cups husked and diced fresh tomatillos
$\frac{1}{2}$ teaspoon fennel seeds
$\frac{1}{2}$ teaspoon cumin seeds
$\frac{1}{2}$ teaspoon coriander seeds
2 teaspoons dried oregano, preferably Mexican
$\frac{1}{4}$ teaspoon ground cinnamon
$1\frac{1}{2}$ cups diced canned tomatoes with their juice
5 cups low-sodium chicken or vegetable broth
2 (15-ounce) cans cannellini or black beans, drained
Kosher salt and freshly ground black pepper
3 tablespoons chopped fresh cilantro leaves
1 ripe avocado, halved and thinly sliced

1. In a medium pot, heat the olive oil over medium heat. Add the onions, poblano chiles, and garlic. Cook until softened but not brown, 3 to 5 minutes.

2. Add the tomatillos, fennel, cumin, coriander, oregano, cinnamon, tomatoes, and broth. Simmer gently for 15 minutes. Add the beans and continue simmering for 10 more minutes. Season to taste with salt and pepper.

3. To serve, ladle the soup into warmed soup bowls. Garnish with chopped cilantro and sliced avocado. Serve immediately.

SWEET CORN CHOWDER WITH CUMIN AND CILANTRO

serves six

Corn chowders come in many varieties, but for a cloudy day, I like mine thick and creamy, with a double chile zing. This version gets uncommon flavor from the freshly toasted spices and whole cobs that are thrown into the pot while the soup simmers. To save time, you can substitute a 12-ounce bag of frozen corn (ideally organic) for fresh corn and dried chiles for fresh jalapeños and poblanos. If you prefer your soup chunky, simply skip the blender step.

2 fresh poblano (or pasilla) chiles
½ teaspoon ground coriander
½ teaspoon ground cumin
2 tablespoons peanut or vegetable oil
3 medium sweet onions, such as Vidalia (or 1½ large yellow onions), diced
½ fresh jalapeño pepper, seeds removed, minced
3 ears white or yellow corn, kernels cut from the cob (about 2 cups), cobs reserved
Kosher salt and freshly ground black pepper
6 cups low-sodium chicken or vegetable broth
1 large bunch fresh cilantro
3 large cloves of roasted garlic (see page 234)
1 cup half-and-half or whole milk
2 to 3 tablespoons fresh lime juice (about 2 limes), or to taste

1. Over a medium flame, char the poblano chiles on all sides until black, about 10 minutes. Place in a small bowl, cover with plastic wrap, and let cool for 5 minutes. Wearing gloves, peel off the charred skin, halve the peppers, and remove the seeds, rinsing with a little water if needed. Chop finely and set aside.

2. In a small, dry skillet, toast the ground coriander and cumin over medium-high heat, stirring, until the spices are fragrant and several shades darker, about 3 minutes. Reserve.

3. In a heavy soup pot, heat the oil over medium heat. Add the onion and cook until softened, stirring frequently, about 6 minutes. Add the jalapeño pepper and 1 cup of the corn kernels and cook over moderate heat, stirring, for about 2 minutes. Add the ground spices and half of the poblanos; season with salt and pepper. Cook, stirring to prevent burning, for 2 minutes.

recipe continues

4. Cut the reserved corn cobs into halves and add with the broth to the pot. Bring the soup to a boil, lower the heat, and simmer uncovered for 30 minutes.

5. Chop a large handful of cilantro leaves and reserve. Tie the remaining sprigs in a bunch with kitchen string and add to the soup while it is simmering.

6. Discard the corn cobs and bunch of cilantro sprigs from the soup. Stir in the roasted garlic along with the half-and-half. Pour the soup into a blender and purée in batches until smooth.

7. Add the lime juice to taste and cook over medium heat, stirring occasionally, until the soup begins to simmer. Add the remaining 1 cup corn and remaining poblanos. Cook, stirring, until heated through, about 3 minutes longer. Serve the chowder in mugs or warmed soup bowls, garnished with the chopped cilantro.

CITRUS-CURED TUNA
WITH PICKLED CARROT
AND RADISH SALAD

serves four

Shutters' version of a tuna ceviche is a frisky combination of thinly sliced raw tuna, pickled carrots, and radishes. Begin this dish the night before serving it for the most flavorful results. When relying on citrus juices to "cook" the tuna, as all ceviches do, only the freshest fish will do. Other firm-fleshed fish may be substituted, such as halibut, yellowtail, or scallops, though the vivid rosiness of tuna gives this dish an especially sexy allure.

1 pound sushi-grade tuna
¼ cup fresh parsley leaves
¼ cup fresh cilantro leaves
2 small shallots, minced
Juice of 1 lemon
Juice of 1 lime
Cracked black peppercorns
12 baby carrots, peeled
2 cups rice vinegar
Large pinch of sugar
1 bunch radishes, stems removed, or 1 hothouse cucumber
Kosher salt
8 ounces tatsoi, mâche, or frisée lettuce, separated into bite-sized leaves
¼ cup grapeseed oil
1 bunch scallions, white and green parts, thinly sliced on the bias

1. In a small glass or ceramic dish, marinate the tuna with the parsley, cilantro, half of the shallots, lemon and lime juices, and pepper. Cover the dish tightly and refrigerate it overnight.

2. Meanwhile, cut the carrots in half lengthwise. Put them in a small glass or ceramic dish and add the rice vinegar, sugar, and remaining shallots.

3. Using a mandoline or sharp knife, thinly slice the radishes. Salt them lightly and add them to the carrots. Cover and marinate in the refrigerator overnight.

4. To serve, drain the tuna and vegetables, reserving ¼ cup of the vegetable marinade. Toss the carrots, radishes, and lettuce in the reserved marinade and the grapeseed oil. Slice the tuna thinly. Arrange a small mound of salad in the middle of each plate and place the tuna slices around it. Season the salad with salt and garnish with the scallions.

HARVEST SALAD OF APPLES, PECANS, AND GOAT CHEESE WITH APPLE VINAIGRETTE

serves six

A reliable salad to pair with almost any main course, this quickly assembled recipe can be tweaked according to your penchant for cheese, nuts, and greens. For variation, I often use Stilton cheese, slivered almonds, and mâche lettuce. Or try feta, pine nuts, and romaine. The apple vinaigrette adds a crisp touch to just about any salad.

APPLE VINAIGRETTE

1 green apple, peeled, cored, and roughly chopped
1 ripe pear, peeled, cored, and roughly chopped
2 tablespoons apple cider vinegar
½ cup apple juice
2 tablespoons fresh lemon juice
½ cup grapeseed oil
Kosher salt and freshly ground black pepper

SALAD

1 head Boston lettuce
1 head frisée lettuce
1 apple, cored and thinly sliced
1 cup pecans, toasted (see page 126) and chopped
6 ounces fresh goat cheese, crumbled

1. Prepare the apple vinaigrette: In a blender, combine the apple, pear, vinegar, apple juice, and lemon juice and purée until smooth. With the machine running, add the oil in a slow stream. Season with salt and pepper. The vinaigrette will keep for up to a week refrigerated.

2. In a large bowl, toss the lettuces, apple, and pecans with some of the vinaigrette. Divide among serving plates and top with the crumbled cheese.

CAESAR SALAD WITH PARMESAN CRISPS

serves six

When clouds loom, I find myself craving this salad. Perhaps its garlicky zing is just the pick-me-up I need when I am slightly bedraggled by the weather. Unlike many Caesars, this one is neither too sharp nor too heavy, thanks to the happy invention of roasted garlic olive oil and the substitution of tofu for egg yolks in the dressing. I usually forgo the standard croutons; the crispy Parmesan tuiles are a decorative flourish that also delivers a flavorful crunch.

Cooking spray
3 ounces freshly grated Parmesan cheese (¾ cup), plus more for serving
Freshly ground black pepper
2 heads romaine lettuce, dark outer leaves removed, washed well and chopped
Eggless Caesar Dressing (page 242)
Garlic Croutons (page 162), optional

1. To make the Parmesan crisps, heat a small nonstick pan over medium heat. When it is hot, spray the pan with a little cooking spray and quickly sprinkle 1½ tablespoons of the cheese in the center. Tap the pan to distribute the cheese evenly over the bottom of the pan; sprinkle with a few grains of black pepper. Cook for just a few minutes, until the cheese is bubbling and golden.

2. Carefully and quickly turn out the cheese disk onto a flat, nonstick surface to cool, or while it is still warm, gently curl it around the handle of a whisk or wooden spoon to create a rounded tuile shape.

3. Repeat the process for each crisp. Once cool, the Parmesan crisps will keep, covered, for up to 3 days.

4. To serve, toss the romaine lightly with the Caesar dressing and extra Parmesan cheese. Top each serving with a Parmesan crisp and croutons, if desired.

WILD MUSHROOM
SALAD WITH TWO DRESSINGS

serves eight

If you love mushrooms, you will adore this elegant salad in which they are sautéed and served warm atop a lively tangle of wild greens. The two dressings, one sweet and light, the other creamy and luscious, play against each other beautifully. This recipe is a lovely way to present even garden-variety white or cremini mushrooms, though wild mushrooms are an exotic treat. You can substitute the corn oil with another unrefined oil, such as avocado, macadamia, or hazelnut.

HONEY-LEMON VINAIGRETTE
2 tablespoons finely chopped shallot
6 tablespoons seasoned rice vinegar
2 tablespoons honey
¼ cup fresh lemon juice (2 small lemons)
½ cup extra-virgin olive oil
Kosher salt and freshly ground black pepper

ROASTED GARLIC–MUSTARD DRESSING
½ cup low-sodium chicken or vegetable broth
2 tablespoons finely chopped shallot
2 cloves of roasted garlic (page 234)
1 tablespoon Dijon mustard
½ cup corn oil
1 teaspoon fresh lemon juice
Kosher salt and freshly ground black pepper

SALAD
1 tablespoon extra-virgin olive oil
**1½ pounds wild mushrooms, such as oyster, chanterelle, or shiitake, cleaned
    (see page 26), sliced if very large**
Kosher salt and freshly ground black pepper
8 cups loosely packed assorted greens (such as arugula, frisée, mizuna, and tatsoi)
Shaved Parmesan cheese, for garnish (optional)

recipe continues

1. Prepare the honey-lemon vinaigrette: In a small bowl, whisk together the shallot, rice vinegar, honey, and lemon juice. Slowly whisk in the olive oil. Adjust the seasoning with salt and pepper to taste. Store in an airtight container in the refrigerator for up to 5 days.

2. Prepare the roasted garlic–mustard dressing: In a medium saucepan over medium heat, bring the broth to a boil and simmer until reduced by half. Cool until just warm. In a blender, combine the shallot, garlic pulp, broth, and mustard; blend until smooth. With the motor running, slowly pour in the oil until the dressing is smooth and thickened. Add the lemon juice and season with salt and pepper. Store in an airtight container in the refrigerator for up to 5 days.

3. To make the salad, in a large sauté pan, heat the oil over medium-high heat. Add the mushrooms and cook until tender and lightly colored but still holding their shape, about 10 minutes. Season with salt and pepper.

4. When the mushrooms are nearly done, lightly toss the greens with some of the honey-lemon vinaigrette and arrange attractively on serving plates. Top with the mushrooms. Spoon the mustard dressing around each plate and garnish with shaved Parmesan cheese, if desired. Serve immediately.

TOASTED PEARL PASTA
WITH ROCK SHRIMP, GREEN BEANS, AND GARLIC

serves six

Also known as Israeli couscous, pearl pasta is so versatile and adorable, it has become one of my favorites. The tiny, soft, roly-poly balls are delightful to present as a side dish or main course. Their toasty mild flavor melds well with almost any bite-sized ingredients and savory broth-based sauce, so if rock shrimp are not your fancy, you can substitute imitation crab, diced cooked fish, chicken, or your favorite vegetables. Served hot, warm, or at room temperature, this dish is even tastier the next day.

6 ounces green beans, trimmed and cut
    into ¼-inch pieces
1¾ cups pearl pasta (10 ounces)
3 tablespoons extra-virgin olive oil
1 large shallot, finely chopped
1½ pounds shelled rock shrimp
2 tablespoons minced garlic

¼ cup low-sodium chicken or vegetable broth
1 cup chopped, seeded tomatoes (about 2 plum tomatoes)
1 cup chopped fresh flat-leaf parsley
⅓ cup chopped fresh basil leaves
Kosher salt and freshly ground black pepper

1. Bring a large pot of salted water to a boil. Have ready a medium bowl of ice water. Cook the green beans until they are tender but still crisp, 6 to 8 minutes. Remove them with a skimmer and plunge into the ice water to stop the cooking (you will need to keep the pot of boiling water for step 3). Drain well in a colander and dry the beans on a kitchen towel. Set aside.

2. In a large, dry skillet over a medium flame, toast the pearl pasta until it is fragrant and lightly colored, 3 to 5 minutes.

3. In the pot of boiling water from step 1, cook the toasted pearl pasta until just tender, about 8 minutes. Drain and reserve in a bowl (do not rinse).

4. Meanwhile, in a large saucepan, heat 1 tablespoon of the olive oil over low heat and sauté the shallot until soft but not colored, 3 to 4 minutes. Increase the heat to medium, add the rock shrimp and garlic, and sauté until the shrimp is opaque, about 3 minutes (if you are using imitation crab or cooked fish or chicken, add them along with the pasta in step 5). Add the broth and continue cooking for another minute or two to reduce slightly.

5. Add the pearl pasta and beans to the shrimp mixture, giving a few tosses to incorporate all the ingredients. Remove from the heat and mix in the remaining 2 tablespoons oil, tomatoes, parsley, basil, and salt and pepper to taste. Transfer to warmed pasta bowls or a serving platter and serve immediately.

STROZZAPRETI WITH SAUSAGE, WHITE BEANS, BROCCOLINI, AND OVEN-DRIED TOMATOES

serves four

One of Shutters' most requested dishes of all time, strozzapreti are long "straws" that drink up the delicious juices from this recipe's savory ingredients. If you can't find strozzapreti, substitute penne, rigatoni, or any pasta you prefer.

2 tablespoons extra-virgin olive oil
8 ounces Italian chicken or vegetarian sausage (2 large links), sliced ½ inch thick
1 shallot, minced
12 pieces Oven-Dried Tomatoes (page 244)
½ cup low-sodium chicken broth
1 (8-ounce) box strozzapreti or other dried pasta
1 bunch broccolini, cut into florets
1 (15-ounce) can white beans, drained
Kosher salt and freshly ground black pepper
¼ cup finely chopped fresh flat-leaf parsley
Freshly shaved Parmesan cheese, for serving

1. Bring a large pot of salted water to a boil.

2. Meanwhile, heat the olive oil in a large skillet over medium-high heat. Add the sausages and cook until browned and cooked through, 5 to 7 minutes. Transfer the sausages to a plate and reserve.

3. Add the shallot to the pan and cook over medium heat, stirring frequently, until fragrant and caramelized, about 5 minutes. Add the tomatoes, reserved sausage slices, and chicken broth; stir until well blended; keep warm.

4. Meanwhile, drop the pasta and broccolini into the boiling water and cook until softened but al dente, about 8 minutes. Drain well and add to the skillet along with the white beans. Over medium heat, toss the ingredients together and heat through for a minute or two, seasoning to taste if necessary (the sausage will most likely provide enough salt for the sauce).

5. Sprinkle with the parsley and serve on a large platter or in warmed pasta bowls, with Parmesan cheese on the side.

SHUTTERS
VEGETARIAN BURGER

makes 6 burgers

Many restaurants appease their vegetarian guests by slapping a frozen vegetable patty on the grill and serving it up burger-style. Not at our boardwalk café. If you take the time to make this veggie burger from scratch, with wholesome ingredients such as brown rice, black beans, and beets, you may even convert some staunch carnivores. Inspired by the superb burger served at Santa Monica's ever-popular restaurant Houston's, our recipe takes less time than the extensive list of ingredients would suggest. This burger deserves an extra-large whole-grain or sprouted-wheat bun.

¼ cup barbecue sauce

2 tablespoons soy sauce

1 tablespoon hoisin sauce

1 tablespoon molasses

1 (15-ounce) can black beans, drained

2 cups cooked brown rice

1 tablespoon oat bran or wheat germ

2 tablespoons finely chopped onion

1 tablespoon minced garlic

2 tablespoons finely chopped cooked beets
  (fresh or canned)

1 tablespoon minced jalapeño pepper, seeded

2 teaspoons extra-virgin olive oil,
  plus additional for cooking

½ teaspoon ground cumin

½ teaspoon chile powder

Kosher salt and freshly ground pepper

1 large egg white, beaten

6 slices Monterey jack or sharp Cheddar cheese

6 whole-grain or sprouted-wheat buns

Shredded lettuce leaves, sliced tomatoes, dill or sweet
  pickles, Sweet Potato Fries (page 135), Louie Dressing
  (page 243), and/or mustard, for garnish

1. In a small container, stir together the barbecue sauce, soy sauce, hoisin sauce, and molasses.

2. In a large bowl, mash the beans with a fork. Stir in 3 tablespoons of the barbecue sauce mixture along with the rice, oat bran, onion, garlic, beets, pepper, oil, cumin, and chile powder. Season to taste with salt and pepper before adding the egg white. Form into 6 patties, each about 1 inch thick. Brush the burgers with the remaining barbecue sauce mixture.

3. Heat a heavy skillet over medium-high heat and add a thin film of oil. Cook the patties until they are well charred on each side, about 4 minutes per side, being careful when flipping them as they fall apart easily. Top them with the cheese and cook until the cheese is melted, about 2 minutes. Transfer the burgers to serving plates.

4. Brown the buns briefly in the skillet. Place them on the serving plates with the burgers and arrange the desired garnishes on the side.

SEARED SEA BASS
WITH BLACK BEAN SAUCE

serves four

The buttery texture of sea bass combined with an exotic, pungent Asian-style black bean sauce makes this dish a perennial favorite at Shutters and at our house. If you can't find sea bass, substitute another mild, boneless fish, such as black cod, red snapper, or John Dory.

8 ounces Chinese fermented black beans (about 2 cups),
   rinsed in water until water runs clear (available at Asian markets and online; see Source Guide)
1½ cups mirin
1¼ cups sake
¼ cup grapeseed or canola oil, plus a small amount for cooking fish
¼ cup minced fresh ginger
2 tablespoons minced garlic
½ cup unseasoned rice vinegar
2½ cups low-sodium chicken or vegetable broth
2 tablespoons sugar
2 teaspoons cornstarch
4 (6- to 8-ounce) skinless sea bass fillets
Kosher salt and freshly ground black pepper
½ bunch scallions (white and green parts), chopped, for garnish

1. Soak the black beans in a small bowl with ½ cup of the mirin and ½ cup of the sake.

2. Meanwhile, in a large saucepan, heat the oil over medium heat and sauté the garlic and ginger until fragrant but not brown, 2 minutes. Add the remaining 1 cup mirin and ¾ cup sake and the rice vinegar. Increase the heat and simmer until the sauce has reduced by half, about 10 minutes.

3. Add the chicken stock and sugar. Return to a simmer, add the beans and their liquid, and continue cooking until the flavors have developed, about 15 minutes.

4. In a small cup, stir together the cornstarch and 2 teaspoons water; stir into the sauce. Simmer another couple minutes, until the sauce has thickened slightly. Remove the sauce from the heat and keep it warm.

5. Pat the fish dry with paper towels and season both sides with salt and pepper. In a large skillet, heat a thin film of oil until almost smoking. Sear the fish until nicely browned on both sides and cooked through, about 4 minutes per side.

6. To serve, spoon a generous pool of black bean sauce onto warmed serving plates. Place the fish on top and sprinkle with the chopped scallions.

ROASTED HALIBUT WITH TOMATO-JUNIPER COMPOTE

serves four

This rendition of the classic Italian fish dish "alla napoletana" is a crisp-topped fillet of halibut with a thick, gin-spiked tomato sauce. For special occasions, I like to serve the fish on a speckled bed of Spinach Risotto (page 163). On weeknights, I dress it down with sides of Tuscan Kale (page 89) and Cowboy Fries (page 184).

10 ripe plum tomatoes, seeded and roughly chopped
2 juniper berries
1 tablespoon dark brown sugar
1 teaspoon kosher salt, plus more for seasoning fish
1 tablespoon gin
3 tablespoons olive oil
4 (6-ounce) skinless halibut (or other thick, white-fleshed fish) fillets
Freshly ground black pepper
Canola oil
4 sprigs fresh basil, for garnish

1. To make the compote, place the tomatoes in a medium bowl. Crush the juniper berries and add to the tomatoes along with the brown sugar, 1 teaspoon salt, and the gin. Set aside to marinate for 30 minutes to 1 hour.

2. Preheat the oven to 350°F.

3. In a stainless-steel saucepan, bring the tomato mixture to a boil, lower the heat, and simmer uncovered until reduced by half, about 10 minutes. Transfer to a blender and slowly add the olive oil while blending. Adjust the seasoning if necessary and keep warm.

4: Pat the fish dry with paper towels and season both sides with salt and pepper. In a large skillet, heat a thin film of canola oil over medium-high heat until almost smoking. Sauté both sides of the fish until nicely colored, about 3 minutes per side. Transfer to the oven to finish cooking, removing the fish when it is just opaque at the thickest part (test with the tip of a knife), 4 to 5 minutes depending on thickness.

5. To serve, ladle a small amount of tomato-juniper compote into 4 warmed serving bowls. Gently place the fish fillets on top, garnish with the fresh basil, and serve.

ROASTED SALMON
with GRAIN MUSTARD
and HERBS

Fish can be comfort food, too, and on a cloudy day, this hearty dish proves it. For a simple, elegant meal, serve the salmon atop a mound of Savoy Cabbage and Spinach (page 88) or Basil Mashed Potatoes (page 182). The sauce has a velvety tart finish and comes together quickly, so before you begin, have your table set and the rest of the meal ready to go.

4 (6-ounce) skinless wild salmon fillets
Kosher salt and freshly ground black pepper
4 tablespoons extra-virgin olive oil
1 medium shallot, finely chopped
⅓ cup fresh lemon juice

½ cup dry white wine
2 teaspoons whole-grain mustard
2 teaspoons chopped fresh dill
2 teaspoons chopped fresh thyme
2 tablespoons chilled unsalted butter, cut into small pieces

1. Preheat the oven to 375°F.

2. Pat the salmon dry with paper towels and season both sides with salt and pepper. Heat 2 tablespoons of the oil in a large ovenproof skillet over medium-high heat until very hot and sear the fish on one side until it is nicely colored, 3 to 4 minutes. Carefully flip the fish over, transfer the skillet to the oven, and roast for about 6 minutes for medium, depending on thickness. The salmon should give slightly to the touch without being firm.

3. Meanwhile, heat the remaining 2 tablespoons oil in a medium saucepan over medium heat. Add the shallot and cook until soft, 3 minutes. Add the lemon juice and white wine, and simmer the sauce for a minute or two, until it has reduced slightly. Whisk in the mustard, dill, and thyme and cook for another minute. Finish the sauce by gradually whisking in the butter, one piece at a time, off the heat. Season to taste with salt and pepper.

4. When the salmon is cooked, transfer the fillets to a warmed platter or serving plates and pour the sauce over the top. Serve immediately.

NOTE
If you prefer your fish grilled, salmon is a fish that certainly cooperates. Simply heat a grill to medium-high heat, brush the seasoned salmon with a little grapeseed oil so that it will not stick, and cook the fish to the desired doneness.

SIX USES FOR A
BUCKET OF SAND

Bring the beach indoors with these simple sand tricks.

Make Beach Votives Fill mismatched glasses halfway with sand, nestle tea lights in the middle, and arrange them copiously around a centerpiece, down the middle of a dining table, throughout the dining area, or in the powder room.

Design a Table Runner Cover the center of a dining table with butcher paper and carefully pour sand down the middle. Decorate the sand with seashells, sand dollars, and plenty of candles. Dim the lights and you have a moonlit beach indoors.

Concoct a Body Scrub In a large bowl, mix 2 parts sifted sand with 1 part each plain yogurt, scented coconut oil, and kosher salt. Lightly scrub the blend over your body in the shower and rinse thoroughly for refreshed, smooth skin.

Collect Sand Souvenirs Fill decorative glass jars with sand and treasures from various beaches you have visited. Secure each jar with a cork and label it with the name of the beach and the date you were there. Display your collection of jars on a mantel or shelf so you can enjoy vacation memories every day.

Play with Sand Clay In an old saucepan, mix 1 cup sand with $\frac{1}{2}$ cup cornstarch and 1 teaspoon cream of tartar. Add $\frac{3}{4}$ cup hot water and cook over medium heat, stirring constantly for a few minutes, until the mixture gets very thick. When it is slightly cooled, children can form the sand clay into castles or sculptures or use molds to shape it into creatures. Decorate the sculptures with toothpick flags, twigs, or other objects while the clay is still damp. Allow several days to dry.

Make Colored Sand Pictures Color sand by mixing it with dry tempera paint. Put it into old spice bottles or shakers. Children can draw images with glue on paper and sprinkle the colored sand onto the glue, shaking off the excess sand when dry.

ROASTED CHICKEN BREASTS WITH CREAMY GRITS

This simple yet soulful dish is the epitome of Southern comfort. The delicious mushroom-shallot sauce gives an earthy hominess to both the chicken and the grits. Serve them on a bed of hearty greens, such as Tuscan Kale (page 89) or Savoy Cabbage and Spinach (page 88) for a terrific down-home dinner. I've even tried cooking salmon in the same way and received rave reviews.

4 (6- to 8-ounce) skin-on boneless
   chicken breast halves
Kosher salt and freshly ground black pepper
1 tablespoon grapeseed oil
2 cups whole milk
2 tablespoons unsalted butter
1 teaspoon minced garlic
Cayenne pepper to taste

½ cup quick-cooking grits
3 ounces grated white Cheddar cheese (¾ cup)
2 small shallots, chopped
2 large portabello mushrooms or 4 ounces
   white mushrooms, diced
½ cup low-sodium rich chicken broth
2 tablespoons chopped fresh flat-leaf parsley,
   for garnish

1. Preheat the oven to 350°F.

2. Season both sides of the chicken liberally with salt and black pepper. In a heavy, ovenproof skillet over medium-high heat, heat the oil until very hot. Add the chicken, skin side down, and allow to cook undisturbed until golden brown, 8 to 10 minutes. Flip the chicken over and transfer the skillet to the oven. Roast the chicken until it is cooked through, about 15 minutes (a meat thermometer should register 160°F).

3. Meanwhile, in a medium saucepan, combine the milk, butter, and garlic. Season with salt and cayenne pepper. Over medium heat, bring the mixture to a boil. Whisk in the grits and cook, whisking occasionally, for about 8 minutes, or until the grits are tender. Stir in the cheese, cover, and keep warm.

4. Remove the chicken from the oven and transfer to a platter to keep warm. Return the skillet to medium heat and add the shallots and mushrooms. Cook, stirring occasionally, until the mushrooms are lightly browned, about 5 minutes. Add the chicken broth and simmer the sauce until it is slightly thickened, about 5 minutes. Season to taste with salt and black pepper.

5. To serve, mound a large spoonful of grits in the center of each serving plate. Place a chicken breast on top of the grits. Spoon the pan sauce over and around the chicken and sprinkle with the parsley.

MEXICAN
POT ROAST

serves six to eight

This aromatic dish gives an unexpected twist to a cold-weather classic. Prepare it the night before or in the morning and let it rest for a couple hours in the refrigerator while you go about your day. Then serve it hot with fresh tortillas, cilantro sprigs, lime wedges, sliced avocados, and crumbled *queso fresco*. If an appetizer is in order, the Tomatillo, Chile, and Bean Chowder (page 59) would be a perfect start.

3 large dried California or New Mexico chiles
   (ancho if available), stemmed and seeded, or
   ¼ cup chile powder
1¾ cups dry red wine
1¼ cups orange juice
¼ cup balsamic or red wine vinegar
2 tablespoons chopped garlic
1 to 2 fresh serrano or jalapeño chiles,
   seeded and minced
2 teaspoons ground cumin

¾ teaspoon ground cinnamon
1 tablespoon chopped fresh oregano leaves or
   1½ teaspoons dried
2 teaspoons kosher salt
2 pounds yellow onions, peeled and thinly sliced
⅔ cup golden raisins or currants
1 (3-pound) center-cut beef brisket, fat trimmed
Warmed tortillas, cilantro sprigs, lime wedges,
   sliced avocados, and crumbled *queso fresco*,
   optional, for serving

1. If using dried chiles, rinse them and place in a saucepan with enough water to cover. Bring to a boil, then remove from the heat, cover, and let stand for 1 hour. Drain and set aside.

2. Preheat the oven to 325°F.

3. In a blender or food processor, purée the softened chiles or chile powder with the wine, orange juice, vinegar, garlic, fresh chiles, cumin, cinnamon, oregano, and salt until smooth.

4. In a large roasting pan, spread half of the onions and raisins on the bottom and place the beef on top of them. Scatter the remaining onions and raisins over the beef and then pour the puréed chile mixture over the top, rubbing it into the meat.

5. Cover the roasting pan tightly and bake until the brisket is fork-tender, 3 to 4 hours, basting often with the pan juices.

6. Remove from the oven and let stand for 20 minutes. Remove the meat from the pan, reserving the onion mixture and pan drippings, and thinly slice across the grain.

7. To serve, place the meat on a platter. Skim the fat from the pan drippings and spoon the drippings over the meat. Serve with the onion mixture on the side and additional garnishes, if desired.

CLOUDYDAYS   83

ROASTED RACK OF LAMB WITH SUN-DRIED CHERRY SAUCE

There's something luxuriously festive about roasted double-bone lamb chops. If you have your butcher trim the extra fat from the bones, they are actually a snap to prepare. Add a luscious cherry sauce flavored with mushrooms, red wine, and port, and you can turn even the gloomiest day into a celebration.

3 eight-bone racks of lamb (each 1¼ to 1½ pounds), rib bones frenched
½ cup extra-virgin olive oil
¼ cup dry white wine
2 teaspoons minced fresh garlic
1 teaspoon minced fresh rosemary or ½ teaspoon dried
1 teaspoon minced fresh thyme or ½ teaspoon dried
1 teaspoon kosher salt
1 teaspoon freshly ground black pepper

SUN-DRIED CHERRY SAUCE
⅛ cup chopped shallots
¾ cup chopped shiitake mushrooms
¾ cup hearty red wine
3 cups low-sodium chicken or beef broth
¼ cup sun-dried cherries
½ teaspoon grated orange zest
¼ cup fresh orange juice
¼ cup ruby port
1 teaspoon chopped fresh thyme leaves
Kosher salt and freshly ground black pepper
Fresh rosemary or thyme sprigs, for garnish

1. To prepare the racks of lamb, use a boning or paring knife to scrape the ribs clean of any residual meat and fat. Trim off the outer layer of fat from the meat, as well as the fatty meat underneath and the silver membrane beneath that.

2. In a large glass baking dish, whisk together the olive oil, wine, garlic, rosemary, thyme, salt, and pepper. Add the lamb, turn to coat, cover, and refrigerate for at least 6 hours or overnight, turning occasionally.

3. Preheat the oven to 425°F. Place a large roasting pan in the oven to preheat.

4. Remove the racks of lamb from the marinade and pat dry with paper towels. Remove the roasting pan from the oven. Transfer the racks, bones pointing up, to the preheated roasting pan. Return to the oven and roast until the racks are medium rare and a thermometer inserted in the center of each rack registers about 125°F, 12 to 15 minutes. Remove the racks to a cutting board, cover the meat loosely with foil, and allow the lamb to rest for 10 minutes before slicing.

5. While the meat is resting, prepare the sun-dried cherry sauce: Pour off 2 tablespoons of the pan drippings from the roasting pan into a large skillet and place over medium heat. Add the shallots and shiitake mushrooms and cook until very lightly browned, about 5 minutes. Add the wine and broth, increase the heat to medium-high, and simmer until reduced by half, about 7 minutes. Add half the cherries and the zest, orange juice, port, and thyme and reduce to a light sauce consistency, about 5 minutes longer. Strain into a small saucepan and add the remaining cherries. Adjust the seasoning with salt and pepper. Keep warm.

6. Cut the racks of lamb into double-bone chops and arrange on warmed serving plates. Spoon the sauce around, garnish with the fresh herb sprigs, and serve immediately.

LEMON-GINGER STRING BEANS

serves six

Transform ho-hum green beans into a spirited side dish with an unexpected kick of lemon zest and fresh ginger. On a blustery day, I like to brown them under the broiler just before serving so the cheese is bubbling and toasty warm.

1 pound string beans or haricots verts, ends trimmed
3 tablespoons extra-virgin olive oil
2 small garlic cloves, minced
2 teaspoons minced fresh ginger
2 teaspoons grated lemon zest
1 tablespoon fresh lemon juice
Kosher salt and freshly ground black pepper
½ cup freshly grated Parmesan cheese
3 tablespoons chopped chives

1. Bring a large pot of salted water to a boil. Have ready a medium bowl filled halfway with ice water. Cook the green beans until tender but still crisp, 6 to 8 minutes. Drain the beans in a colander and plunge into the ice water to stop the cooking. Drain well again and dry them on a kitchen towel.

2. In a large skillet, heat the olive oil over medium-low heat. Add the garlic, ginger, and lemon zest. Cook until fragrant but not brown, about 5 minutes.

3. Add the beans and sauté for a few minutes, until the beans are hot and coated with oil. Add the lemon juice and season with salt and pepper to taste. Sprinkle with the Parmesan cheese and chopped chives and serve immediately.

SAVOY CABBAGE AND SPINACH

serves four to six

The light and dark greens of this versatile, year-round side dish make a lovely bed for any piece of fish or chicken. In the spring and summer months, try adding petite peas for another shade of color and texture. (Frozen organic peas are fine, but add them toward the end of the cooking to preserve their vivid color.) If you can find smoked salt (see Source Guide), the dish will be even more beguiling. (See photograph, page 86.)

2 tablespoons extra-virgin olive oil
2 tablespoons butter
2 cups shredded savoy cabbage (about $\frac{1}{2}$ small head)
2 cups baby spinach leaves
Salt (preferably smoked) and freshly ground black pepper

In a large sauté pan, heat the olive oil and butter over medium heat. Add the cabbage and spinach and, stirring occasionally, cook until they have wilted, about 10 minutes. Season to taste with salt and pepper.

TUSCAN
KALE

Tuscan kale (also known as *cavolo nero*) is a dark-leaved, often ignored relative of cabbage that hangs around produce displays in the winter, long after other greens have disappeared. It is robust and wholesome, yet its slightly sharp edge needs to be tamed with a bit of sweetness (in this case, shallots) and patient cooking. Regular kale can be prepared in the same manner. (See photograph, page 86.)

2 tablespoons extra-virgin olive oil
2 small shallots, minced
1 bunch Tuscan kale (about 1 pound), stemmed and coarsely chopped
½ cup low-sodium chicken or vegetable broth, or more if needed
Kosher salt and freshly ground black pepper

1. In a large, deep skillet, heat the olive oil over medium heat. Add the shallots and kale and cook until the kale has wilted, about 5 minutes.

2. Add the broth, cover, and continue cooking, stirring occasionally, until the kale is tender, 20 to 30 minutes. Add more broth or water if necessary to cook the greens completely, then uncover and boil off any excess liquid. Season to taste with salt and pepper and serve.

BUTTERMILK ONION RINGS

The key to crispy, crunchy onion rings is in the frying. The oil must be hot enough every time you add a batch of onion rings, and there should be enough of it so that the batter has room to puff up as the onions cook. As with any fried food, the sooner you can get these on the table, the better. But you can also spread them on a baking sheet and keep them warm in a 250°F oven until ready to serve.

2 quarts vegetable oil (such as grapeseed or peanut), for frying
2 large yellow onions, peeled and left whole
2 cups buttermilk
Kosher salt and freshly ground black pepper
1 cup all-purpose flour

1. Heat the oil (about 4 inches) in a large, heavy pot or deep fryer to approximately 365°F.

2. Slice the onions into ¼-inch-thick rings. Place them in a large bowl and cover with the buttermilk. Season with salt and pepper.

3. Place the flour in a shallow dish and season with salt and pepper. Dip the onion rings into the seasoned flour, then dip them again in the buttermilk and again in the seasoned flour (this will be a messy process).

4. Test the oil by dropping a small amount of batter into the hot oil—it should sizzle and brown quickly. Fry the onion rings in small batches until they are golden, 2 to 3 minutes. Let the oil come back to temperature before frying the next batch.

5. Remove the onion rings with a slotted metal spoon and drain them on paper towels. Sprinkle them with a little extra salt if needed.

6. Pile the onion rings in a tall stack on a serving plate and serve them immediately.

APPLE-CINNAMON CRISP

Most people are quite happy when presented with any warm, bubbling, golden-topped fruit dessert. This recipe is technically a crisp, but its juicy filling reminds me of a cobbler or betty. Designed to showcase fall's best apples, the homespun treat tastes best made with a combination of organic Granny Smith and Braeburn varieties, which when cooked retain their tangy punch without getting mushy. This recipe will also turn out beautifully with pears (I prefer Comice, Anjou, and Bosc).

4 cups peeled, cored, and sliced apples (about 6 apples)
1 teaspoon ground cinnamon
¼ teaspoon kosher salt
1 cup sugar
½ cup (1 stick) butter, plus more for greasing baking dish
¾ cup all-purpose flour
Whipped cream or ice cream, for serving, optional

1. Preheat the oven to 350°F.

2. Grease a 10-inch, deep pie dish or large soufflé dish. Fill with the apple slices and sprinkle with the cinnamon and salt, tossing to distribute evenly. Pour ½ cup water over the apples.

3. In a small bowl, combine the sugar, butter, and flour using your fingertips or a pastry blender until crumbly. Sprinkle the topping over the apples.

4. Bake until the apples are bubbling and the topping is browned, 40 to 45 minutes. Serve warm, either plain or with whipped cream or ice cream on the side, if desired. (The dessert can also be baked the night before or in the morning, refrigerated, and reheated in a 350°F oven for 15 minutes, until warm and bubbly.)

ESSENTIALLY EFFORTLESS
ENTERTAINING TIPS

What makes for a simple, chic affair? A playful table, delicious casual food, and a breezy vibe will ensure a good time for everyone. If you think this is easier said than done, here are a few tips to help you let your hair down.

Remember your purpose Remind yourself the reason you decided to gather your friends in the first place: their good company. No need to impress; being yourself is the key to putting everyone at ease.

Know your audience With all of the quirky eaters out there (some of my best friends, in fact), it's impossible to please every palate. When I invite friends over, I always ask if they have any allergies or food preferences and plan accordingly. It can get complicated, but the surest way to spoil your time is to watch one of your guests sheepishly pushing food around his or her plate. It is better to surprise your guests with a low-fat or meatless menu than have one disappointed guest.

Prep in advance Choose dishes that can be made ahead of time and try to finish your preparations at least two hours before your guests arrive, so you have time to relax. Stay away from fussy dishes that keep you sequestered in the kitchen and away from company. I like to leave last-minute salad tossing and bread slicing to those dear guests who are keen on being helpful.

Serve family-style Have guests serve themselves from an assortment of hand-painted platters, various-shaped trays, and colorful bowls. For your more curious guests, they can spark conversation. (In my eclectic mix of serving pieces collected while traveling, nothing quite matches, but everything has a story.) At the very least, having everyone passing plates and helping serve adds a little more exuberance to your meals.

Enforce quality control Taste and smell every dish you will be serving to make sure it is appealing, especially when serving fish. This way you can avoid an embarrassing moment like the one I had when I unwittingly served a day-too-old fish to twelve guests. If you are not sure about the freshness of the fish, cook a tiny piece as a test.

Amp up the ambiance Select your favorite music in advance and make sure it is playing when your guests arrive. I like to turn up the volume and tempo as the meal progresses so the mood is upbeat when it is time to say good-bye.

Finally . . . A little laughter can go a long way to making an ordinary meal magical!

LEMON TART

I love this tart for its confident, one-note approach to dessert. But if you choose to embellish it, Fresh Raspberry Sauce (page 145) is the perfect harmony. The tart can be made a day ahead, refrigerated, and served cold.

5 large eggs
2 large egg yolks
Grated zest of 1 lemon
½ cup fresh lemon juice
1½ cups sugar
¾ cup (1½ sticks) unsalted butter, cut into 6 pieces
1 packet unflavored gelatin, softened in ¼ cup water
1 prebaked 9-inch piecrust

1. Bring 2 inches of water to a boil in a medium pot over medium heat.

2. Meanwhile, in a large mixing bowl, mix the eggs, yolks, lemon zest, lemon juice, and sugar. Place over the pot of boiling water and, whisking constantly, cook until the mixture thickens and has tripled in volume, about 10 minutes.

3. Remove the lemon mixture from the heat and whisk in the butter and softened gelatin.

4. Pour the filling into the piecrust. Set aside to cool, then refrigerate for at least 2 hours or overnight.

5. Preheat the broiler. Just before serving, place the tart under the broiler for a couple minutes, until the surface is golden and bubbling. Slice and serve.

PEACH-BLACKBERRY CRUMBLE

serves six

A fruit crumble is the perfect comfort dish to end a cloudy day—or any day. This is a low-fat version featuring two stars of the summer season, peaches and blackberries. During fall or winter, when they are not available, use fresh plums, apples, pears, or defrosted frozen fruit. You can also add dried cranberries or chopped nuts for a bit of texture. I like to serve the crumble topped with ice cream on warmer days or a dollop of crème fraîche and a drizzle of Caramel Sauce (page 249) on colder days. For an elegant touch, serve individual crumbles in small soufflé cups (reduce the baking time by 10 to 15 minutes).

FRUIT

4 large ripe peaches (about 2 pounds),
   peeled (see opposite), pitted, and sliced
½ pint fresh blackberries
¼ cup sugar
1 tablespoon cornstarch
1 teaspoon grated lemon zest

TOPPING

½ cup quick-cooking oats
¼ cup firmly packed brown sugar
⅓ cup all-purpose flour
¼ teaspoon ground nutmeg
½ teaspoon ground cinnamon
¼ teaspoon kosher salt
2 tablespoons cold unsalted butter or margarine

1. Preheat the oven to 375°F. Grease an 8-inch square glass or ceramic baking dish.

2. Arrange the peaches in the baking dish and scatter the blackberries on top. Stir the sugar and cornstarch together and sprinkle over the fruit, followed by the lemon zest.

How to Peel Peaches

Bring a medium pot of water to a boil.
Meanwhile, using a sharp paring knife,
cut a small *x* into the skin on the bottom
of each peach. Drop the peaches gently
into the boiling water. When the skin
begins to curl up around the *x*, after 1
to 2 minutes, remove the peaches from
the water with a skimmer. When they are
cool enough to handle, use the paring
knife to gently peel away the skins.

3. To make the topping, in a medium bowl, toss together the oats, brown sugar, flour, nutmeg, cinnamon, and salt, cutting in the butter using your fingers or a pastry cutter until the mixture is crumbly. Sprinkle the topping over the fruit.

4. Bake for about 50 minutes, or until the topping is golden and the filling is bubbling underneath. Serve hot. (The dessert can also be baked the night before or in the morning, refrigerated, and reheated in a 350°F oven for 15 minutes, until warm and bubbly.)

MALTED CHOCOLATE CREAM PIE

serves eight

Even life at the beach can have its challenging moments, especially when the weather, traffic, or kids won't cooperate. Present this dreamy ode to chocolate and magically, happy moods are restored. Rich and unapologetic, it is like a fudgy, flourless chocolate cake with a vanilla-scented cloud of cream on top.

PIE AND FILLING

1½ cups heavy cream

1 cup whole milk

1 cup malt powder (such as Horlicks)

8 ounces milk chocolate, chopped

8 ounces extra-bitter chocolate, chopped

2 large eggs

1 prebaked Chocolate Piecrust (page 248)

TOPPING

1½ cups heavy cream

½ cup mascarpone cheese

¼ cup sugar

1 tablespoon vanilla extract

Cocoa powder, for dusting

1. Prepare the filling: In a large saucepan, combine the cream and milk and bring just to a boil. Put the malt powder in a small bowl. Ladle a little hot cream mixture into the malt powder and whisk until smooth. Add this mixture to the cream mixture in the pan and whisk until incorporated. Remove the pan from the heat.

2. Add the chocolates to the pan, let stand for about 5 minutes, and then whisk to combine. Whisk in the eggs, one at a time, until the mixture is smooth. Strain into a medium container and set aside or refrigerate until ready to use, or for up to 2 days.

3. Preheat the oven to 300°F.

4. Fill the piecrust with the filling (it should come just up to the edge of the crust). Bake for 10 minutes, rotate the pie, and then bake for 7 to 10 minutes more. The edges of the filling should be puffed and set, while the middle is still slightly loose. Let the pie cool, then refrigerate for at least 1 hour or overnight.

5. Prepare the topping: Using a whisk or an electric mixer, whip the cream, mascarpone, sugar, and vanilla to stiff peaks. Refrigerate until needed or for up to 4 hours.

6. To assemble, carefully unmold the pie from the tart pan. Scoop the topping onto the center of the pie. Slice the pie, sprinkle each slice with a little cocoa powder, and serve.

STRAWBERRY SHORTCAKE

The charm of this mainstay dessert is its simplicity. Essentially a buttery scone filled with fresh strawberry compote, this recipe could even double as a breezy breakfast dish (trade the whipped cream for vanilla yogurt). To serve it for a crowd, prepare the shortcake dough and strawberry compote up to a week ahead and simply bake and assemble the shortcakes at the last minute.

3 cups all-purpose flour

½ cup plus 2 tablespoons granulated sugar, plus more for sprinkling

1½ tablespoons baking powder

½ teaspoon kosher salt

½ cup (1 stick) unsalted butter, chilled, cut into small cubes

2 large eggs

¾ cup chilled heavy cream, plus more for brushing

2 pints strawberries, hulled

Juice of 2 lemons

Confectioners' sugar, for serving

Whipped cream or vanilla ice cream, for serving

1. In an electric mixer or large bowl, combine the flour, ½ cup of the granulated sugar, the baking powder, salt, and butter. Mix until the consistency is crumbly.

2. Add the eggs and cream. Mix until just combined, being careful not to overmix. Gather the dough, cover with plastic wrap, and let rest in the refrigerator for at least 1 hour or up to 3 days.

3. Preheat the oven to 400°F.

4. In a blender or food processor, purée half of the strawberries with the lemon juice and the remaining 2 tablespoons granulated sugar, adding more to taste if necessary. Strain through a fine sieve; reserve or refrigerate for up to 1 week.

5. On a lightly floured surface, roll out the dough to 1 inch thick and cut with a 3-inch round cutter into 8 circles. Brush the tops lightly with cream and sprinkle with granulated sugar. Transfer to a parchment-lined baking sheet and bake until puffed and golden brown, about 12 minutes. Remove from the oven and allow to cool for a few minutes.

6. To serve, slice the remaining strawberries in half and toss them with the strawberry sauce. Slice the shortcakes in half and place a top and bottom on each serving plate. Spoon the strawberry mixture over the bottom half and lean the other half on top. Sprinkle with confectioners' sugar and garnish with a large dollop of whipped cream or a scoop of ice cream.

BERRIES WITH CHOCOLATE-COCONUT FONDUE

serves eight

You don't need a fondue pot to serve this sure bet of a dessert. In fact, you don't even need fresh berries, as this warm pool of tropical-scented chocolate is delicious for dunking any kind of fresh or dried fruit, cookies, cubes of angel food or pound cake, or marshmallows. If you do happen to have a fondue pot, this dessert becomes extra cozy, especially to cap a chilly afternoon or frosty evening.

1 (15-ounce) can sweetened cream of coconut (like Coco Lopez)
12 ounces bittersweet or semisweet chocolate, finely chopped
¼ cup heavy cream
½ teaspoon coconut extract
4 cups mixed berries, such as strawberries, blackberries, and raspberries

1. Combine the cream of coconut and chocolate in a heavy saucepan. Stir constantly over very low heat until the chocolate melts and the mixture is smooth, about 5 minutes.

2. Stir in the cream and coconut extract, and cook until warmed through, another minute or so. Transfer the mixture to 8 small ceramic ramekins or a fondue pot.

3. To serve, arrange the berries alongside the warm fondue, with skewers on the side for dipping the fruit into the chocolate. (The fondue can be prepared a couple hours ahead and stored covered at room temperature. It can also be stored in the refrigerator for up to 1 week. To rewarm the fondue, microwave it briefly, stirring halfway through, or warm it over very low heat, stirring constantly to prevent burning.)

BALMYNIGHTS

In summer and early fall, there are magical days at the beach, when the afternoon heat lingers into the night and a salty effervescence floats in the evening air. Relish them as long as possible. Lose the daytime beach clothes for a flirty floral dress or impractical white trousers. Linger over dinner, kick off your shoes, and stretch out. There is no reason to rush a balmy night, especially with plenty of ways to savor it in style.

Great food can only add to a sultry evening, and there are ample recipes to inspire your menu. Colorful salads with lots of verve, fresh and flavorful fish dishes, and meatless main courses are light ways to bring on the night. Finish with the simplest of desserts—maybe a scoop of vanilla bean ice cream with Fresh Raspberry Sauce. After all, holding on to what's sweet and seasonal is what balmy nights are all about.

BALMYNIGHTS

Sunset Cocktails: Pomegranate Martini, Mai Tai, On the Boardwalk
Margarita, A Day at the Beach, Sex on the Beach, Shutters Sky-Blue

Ciabatta with Fresh Pesto and Ricotta Cheese

Chilled Avocado-Corn Soup with Cilantro Oil

Mediterranean Salad

Lobster Salad with Mango, Papaya, Cucumber,
Avocado, and Lime-Mint Vinaigrette

Dungeness Crab Salad with Honey-Tangerine Vinaigrette

Sliced Lamb Loin Salad with Cucumbers,
Tomatoes, and Crumbled Feta Cheese

Grilled Vegetables with Fluffy Couscous

Barley Risotto with Carrot-Corn Broth

Seared Whitefish with Sweet Corn, Kohlrabi, and Tomato Compote

Roasted Halibut with Fennel-Tomato Sauce

Seared Salmon with Artichokes, Salsify, and Saffron Broth

Grilled Turkey Burgers

Sweet Potato Fries

Roasted Pepper and Corn Succotash

Strawberry-Rhubarb Cobbler

Yogurt Mousse with Honey-Poached Apricots

Lemon Curd with Fresh Blackberries

Passion Fruit Crème Brûlée

Chocolate Mango Semifreddo

Fresh Raspberry Sauce

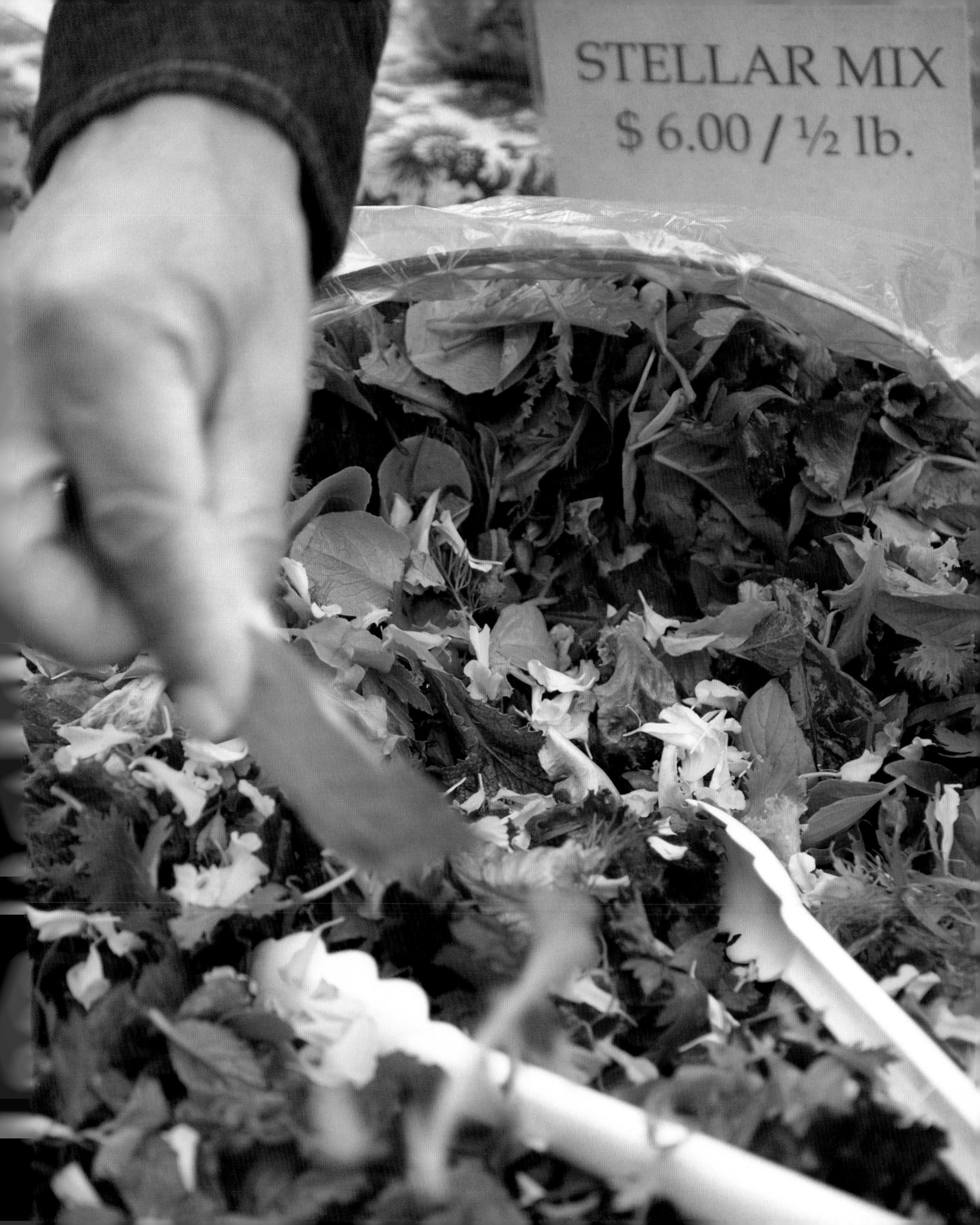
STELLAR MIX
$ 6.00 / ½ lb.

SUNSET COCKTAILS

Greet your guests with something deliciously icy and let the good vibrations flow! Here are the top six most popular cocktails at Shutters (and now at my house). I've given you the measurements traditionally in ounces but also in cups and tablespoons in case you do not have a jigger handy.

POMEGRANATE MARTINI

Pomegranate syrup and rose water are available at Middle Eastern markets and specialty gourmet stores (see Source Guide). You can substitute pomegranate juice, which is just as refreshing but less concentrated (for this recipe, use about ½ cup).

2 ounces (¼ cup) Absolut Citron vodka or other lemon-flavored vodka
½ ounce (1 tablespoon) fresh lemon juice
½ ounce (1 tablespoon) pomegranate syrup
Ice
Dash of rose water, optional
Twist of lemon, for garnish

serves one

In a cocktail shaker, shake the vodka, lemon juice, and pomegranate syrup vigorously with ice, then strain into a chilled martini glass. Add a dash of rose water, if desired. Garnish with a twist of lemon.

MAI TAI

2 ounces (¼ cup) dark rum
2 ounces (¼ cup) fresh orange juice
2 ounces (¼ cup) pineapple juice
Ice
Dash of grenadine syrup
Orange wedge, for garnish

serves one

In a cocktail shaker, shake the rum and juices with ice, then strain into a highball glass filled with ice. Garnish with a dash of grenadine syrup and a wedge of orange.

ON THE BOARDWALK
MARGARITA

serves one

Lime wedge
Coarse salt
2 ounces (¼ cup) tequila
1 ounce (2 tablespoons) Grand Marnier or Cointreau
2 ounces (¼ cup) fresh lemonade
1 ounce (2 tablespoons) fresh orange juice

Rub the edge of a cocktail glass with the lime wedge, then dip the glass into a saucer filled with coarse salt. In a cocktail shaker with ice, combine the tequila, Grand Marnier, lemonade, and orange juice. Shake well and strain into the salted cocktail glass. Garnish with the lime wedge.

A DAY at the BEACH

Ice
1 ounce (2 tablespoons) coconut rum
½ ounce (1 tablespoon) Amaretto liqueur
4 ounces (½ cup) fresh orange juice
½ ounce (1 tablespoon) grenadine
1 strawberry, for garnish

In a cocktail shaker filled with ice, shake the rum, Amaretto, and orange juice. Strain into a highball glass filled with ice. Add the grenadine and garnish with a strawberry.

SEX on the BEACH

Ice   serves one
1½ ounces (3 tablespoons) vodka
½ ounce (1 tablespoon) peach schnapps
¼ ounce (½ tablespoon) Chambord
2 ounces (¼ cup) cranberry juice
2 ounces (¼ cup) pineapple juice
Pineapple or orange slice, for garnish

In a cocktail shaker filled with ice, shake the vodka, schnapps, Chambord, and juices well; strain into a chilled highball glass. Garnish with a pineapple or orange slice.

SHUTTERS SKY-BLUE

Ice   serves one
2½ ounces (⅓ cup) Absolut Mandarin or other citrus-flavored vodka
1 ounce (2 tablespoons) fresh lemonade
¼ ounce (½ tablespoon) Blue Curaçao
Splash of Sprite
Lemon or orange slice, for garnish

In a cocktail shaker filled with ice, shake the vodka, lemonade, Curaçao, and Sprite well; strain into a chilled martini glass. Garnish with a slice of lemon or orange.

BEACH BAR ESSENTIALS

All you need to know to become a great domestic bartender is how to master a few impressive drinks. There is no need to stock your bar with a bonanza of alcohol. When I entertain, usually my guests will politely ask, "What are you drinking?" or "What's open?," leaving me the opportunity to offer them whatever is on tap. For dinner parties, I usually make a "house cocktail"—something colorful with a tantalizing name—and present it as guests arrive. Invariably, guests will opt for the enticing drink or else choose something tamer like wine or water. Here are some more tricks of the beach-bar trade:

Start collecting attractive glassware
The pieces needn't be costly or crystal, or even form a large matching set. Your collection should include champagne flutes, highballs (tall with straight sides), rocks (old-fashioned) glasses, and a few large tumblers for blended drinks.

Buy in bulk
Most name-brand (expensive) alcohol is available in large jugs at Costco and other discount superstores. Premix your cocktail du jour and pour it into an attractive pitcher. Your guests will never know your thrifty bar secrets!

Use large ice cubes
Small cubes or shavings water down drinks.

Garnish glasses or pitchers
Some of my favorite garnishes are slices of grapefruit and blood orange, fresh mint sprigs, pomegranate seeds, olives on jeweled cocktail sticks, and frozen cranberries, raspberries, or peach slices, which help keep cocktails cold.

CIABATTA WITH FRESH PESTO AND RICOTTA CHEESE

serves four

This addictive hors d'oeuvre is a sure way to make a basket of crusty ciabatta bread disappear. The creamy ricotta cheese tempers the garlicky bite of the pesto, though you could easily substitute a mild goat cheese. To add another interesting dimension, try different variations for the basil, such as mint or spinach, and the nuts, such as walnuts, pistachios, or almonds. The pesto is also delicious with raw or roasted vegetables, breadsticks, roasted potatoes, or, of course, tossed with pasta.

2 cups packed fresh basil leaves
¼ cup freshly grated Parmesan cheese
3 tablespoons pine nuts, toasted (see page 126) and cooled
3 garlic cloves
½ cup extra-virgin olive oil
1 loaf ciabatta or other crusty bread, thinly sliced
8 ounces fresh whole-milk or part-skim ricotta cheese

1. Combine the basil leaves, Parmesan cheese, nuts, and garlic in a food processor fitted with the metal blade and pulse until the leaves are minced finely. Add the olive oil and pulse to blend, stopping to scrape down the sides of the bowl. Transfer the pesto to an airtight container and cover it with a thin layer of olive oil to keep it from browning. Store covered in the refrigerator for up to 1 week, or freeze in resealable plastic bags for up to 2 months.

2. Warm the ciabatta in a toaster oven or oven and place it in a bread basket. Fill a shallow dish with the pesto and drop spoonfuls of ricotta cheese on top.

CHILLED AVOCADO-CORN SOUP WITH CILANTRO OIL

serves four

This smooth, subtly flavored soup is delicate enough to precede a multicourse meal and casual enough for a picnic. Make it a couple days ahead, and the rich flavors of avocado, sweet corn, and lime will bloom even more. The cilantro oil adds a swirl of finesse with minimal fuss.

CILANTRO OIL
1 cup coarsely chopped fresh cilantro leaves
¼ cup extra-virgin olive oil
½ teaspoon kosher salt

SOUP
1 ear corn, husks removed
1 quart low-sodium vegetable broth
1 garlic clove, smashed
1 medium white onion, chopped
Kosher salt
2 firm but ripe avocados, peeled and pitted
3 tablespoons fresh lime juice
¼ cup sour cream

1. Prepare the cilantro oil: In a blender or small food processor, purée the cilantro, oil, and salt. Pour the mixture into a fine-mesh sieve set over a bowl and let it drain for 15 minutes. Store the oil in an airtight container at room temperature for up to 5 days.

2. Heat a dry, heavy cast-iron skillet over medium-high heat and roast the whole corn, turning occasionally, until charred in spots, about 10 minutes. Transfer the corn to a cutting board and, when cool enough to handle, cut the kernels from the cob. Cut the cob into thirds.

3. Bring the kernels, cob pieces, broth, garlic, onion and 1½ teaspoons of salt to a boil in a large saucepan and boil until the liquid is reduced to about 3 cups, about 20 minutes. Remove from the heat and cool, uncovered. Discard the cob pieces.

recipe continues

4. In a blender, purée the corn mixture. Add 1 of the avocados and 2 tablespoons of the lime juice to the blender; purée until smooth. Season to taste with salt. Transfer to a container, cover the surface of the soup with plastic wrap, and then cover the container with plastic wrap. Chill the soup for at least 1 hour, until very cold.

5. To serve, use a small melon-ball scoop to make balls of the remaining avocado or simply dice it into small cubes. In a small bowl, toss the avocado gently with the remaining tablespoon of lime juice. Ladle the soup into 4 chilled, shallow soup bowls. Divide the avocado among the bowls, then drizzle each with a little sour cream (thin if necessary with a little water or lime juice) and a swirl of cilantro oil.

MEDITERRANEAN SALAD

serves four

A tasty twist on the ubiquitous grilled-vegetable salad that has made its way onto so many L.A. restaurant menus, this salad is one of my favorite ways to use leftover grilled vegetables or chicken. With a baked potato or some good crusty bread, it is a meal in itself.

2 cups diced assorted grilled vegetables (see page 122)
4 cups baby greens
½ medium red onion, very thinly sliced
8 ounces salami or leftover grilled chicken, cut into ¼-inch strips, optional
¼ cup kalamata or niçoise olives
Oven-Dried Tomato Vinaigrette (page 241)
8 ounces mozzarella cheese, cut into ¼-inch strips
Kosher salt and freshly ground black pepper

Toss the grilled vegetables in a large bowl with the greens, onion, salami, olives, and a little vinaigrette. Top with the mozzarella cheese and season to taste with salt and pepper. Transfer to a serving bowl or plates and serve immediately.

LOBSTER SALAD WITH MANGO, PAPAYA, CUCUMBER, AVOCADO, AND LIME-MINT VINAIGRETTE

serves four as a first course

The lovely thing about lobster is that it doesn't require much adornment. This salad is pretty and straightforward, with a refreshing vinaigrette that unites all the tropical elements. I recommend buying precooked lobsters from a reliable local seafood merchant. To test the precooked lobster for freshness, pull its tail out straight; if it snaps back into a curl, it is fresh. If it does not, the meat will not be nearly as tender or sweet. The lobster tail can be left whole and served in its shell for a more dramatic presentation. If you don't do shellfish, use grilled salmon instead.

1 large precooked whole lobster
1 English cucumber, peeled, cut into $\frac{1}{2}$ × 3-inch batons
1 head butter lettuce, leaves torn into large pieces
Lime-Mint Vinaigrette (page 240)
1 mango, peeled, pitted, and sliced
1 papaya, peeled, seeded, and sliced
1 firm but ripe avocado, peeled, pitted, and sliced
Kosher salt and freshly ground black pepper
Chopped fresh herbs, such as basil or mint, for garnish
Salmon caviar, for garnish, optional

1. With a sharp knife, carefully cut off the lobster tail where it joins the body. Break off the claws, legs, and feelers. Using the knife, split the body in half lengthwise and remove the red coral and liver, reserving the coral for garnish. Remove the tail meat and the black vein; slice the meat on the bias into 1-inch-thick pieces. Crack the claws and knuckles and remove the meat from them. Keep the lobster meat chilled until ready to serve.

2. To assemble, stir the reserved lobster coral into $\frac{1}{2}$ cup of the vinaigrette and use to lightly dress the cucumber and butter lettuce. Arrange on serving plates or a platter with the mango, papaya, and avocado slices. Place the slices of lobster on top of the salad, season with salt and pepper, and drizzle with additional vinaigrette to taste. Serve chilled, garnished with herbs and a spoonful of salmon caviar, if desired.

DUNGENESS CRAB SALAD WITH HONEY-TANGERINE VINAIGRETTE

serves four as an appetizer

The most popular of the West Coast crabs, the Dungeness is seasonally available up and down our coast. But there are countless other varieties of crabs that hail from all waters, so choose your favorite local variety for this easy and delicious salad. Just make sure you pick through the meat carefully with your fingers to remove any stray bits of grit and shell.

16 ounces lump crabmeat
¼ cup diced red bell pepper
2 tablespoons mayonnaise or Basic Aïoli (page 235)
2 tablespoons fresh lemon juice
4 cups assorted baby greens
Kosher salt and freshly ground black pepper
Honey-Tangerine Vinaigrette (page 240)
1 grapefruit, sectioned
1 tangerine, sectioned

1. In a medium bowl, combine the crabmeat, diced bell pepper, mayonnaise, and lemon juice. Mix together gently.

2. To serve, arrange the greens on serving plates. Divide the crab salad on top of the greens, season with salt and pepper to taste, and drizzle with the vinaigrette to taste. Arrange the grapefruit and tangerine sections around the salads.

SLICED LAMB LOIN SALAD
WITH CUCUMBERS, TOMATOES, AND CRUMBLED FETA CHEESE

serves four

On the nights that you can't decide between a light and virtuous salad and a nourishing protein fix, this recipe comes to the rescue. Mediterranean inspired, it will also marry well with grilled steak or fish.

2 teaspoons grapeseed oil
1 pound boneless lamb loin
Kosher salt and freshly ground black pepper
4 cups mixed baby greens
1 English cucumber, peeled and diced
3 medium tomatoes, cut into wedges
½ red onion, thinly sliced
½ cup pitted kalamata or niçoise olives, halved
Red Wine Vinaigrette (page 239)
8 ounces feta cheese, crumbled, optional

1. Heat a medium skillet over high heat until very hot. Add the grapeseed oil and swirl to coat the bottom. Season the lamb loin generously with salt and pepper and add it to the pan. Sear the lamb until well browned on all sides and medium rare inside, about 8 to 10 minutes. Transfer to a cutting board, cover loosely with foil, and let rest for 10 minutes before slicing thinly.

2. In a large bowl, toss the greens, cucumber, tomato wedges, onion, and olives with about ⅓ cup of the vinaigrette (or more to taste). Arrange a mound of salad on each serving plate and top with slices of lamb. Garnish with the feta cheese, if desired.

GRILLED VEGETABLES
WITH FLUFFY COUSCOUS

Anyone can go vegetarian with this naturally colorful and fragrant dish. Because of its universal appeal, it's perfect for a large luncheon, dinner party, or buffet. For optimal flavor, use organic vegetables if available.

GRILLED VEGETABLES
1 red bell pepper, halved and seeded
1 green bell pepper, halved and seeded
1 medium zucchini, sliced ½ inch thick on the bias
1 medium yellow squash, sliced ½ inch thick on the bias
1 Japanese eggplant, sliced ½ inch thick on the bias
1 medium carrot, sliced ¼ inch thick on the bias
1 bunch thick asparagus, tough ends trimmed
Balsamic Vinaigrette (page 238) or Oven-Dried
   Tomato Vinaigrette (page 241)
Kosher salt and freshly ground black pepper

FLUFFY COUSCOUS
1 tablespoon unsalted butter
1 small shallot, minced
1 garlic clove, minced
2 cups low-sodium chicken or vegetable broth
1 (10-ounce) box whole-wheat or regular couscous

1. In a large bowl, toss the peppers, zucchini, squash, eggplant, carrot, and asparagus with the vinaigrette and set aside to marinate for at least 10 minutes or up to 4 hours.

2. Preheat a grill on high heat.

3. Make the couscous: In a medium saucepan, heat the butter over medium heat. Add the shallot and garlic and cook until soft, 3 minutes. Add the broth and bring to a boil. Turn off the heat, add the couscous, cover, and let stand for 5 minutes, or until the couscous has absorbed all the liquid. Uncover and fluff with a fork; keep warm.

4. Remove the vegetables from the marinade, reserving a little marinade for serving. Grill the vegetables until well marked and soft, about 10 minutes. Season them to taste with salt and pepper.

5. To serve, spoon the couscous onto warmed serving plates or a large platter and mound the grilled vegetables on top. Drizzle with the reserved vinaigrette and serve.

NOTE
To make this a complete meal for a vegetarian, add 6 ounces of sliced extra-firm tofu per person to the vegetable marinade and grill it along with the vegetables.

BARLEY RISOTTO
WITH CARROT-CORN BROTH

serves six

When it comes to risotto, creaminess is key, but it doesn't have to come from a chunk of butter. This risotto gets its richness from a luminous orange broth infused with the sweetness of carrots and corn. The barley — used in place of Arborio rice — lends extra texture as well as heart-healthy fiber, while tomatillos, cumin, and cilantro give this unique dish a Southwestern twist. The risotto may be prepared up to step 5 a day ahead and refrigerated.

5 to 6 cups low-sodium vegetable broth
¼ cup extra-virgin olive oil
1 medium yellow onion, minced
2 garlic cloves, sliced into slivers
1½ cups pearl barley
1 teaspoon whole cumin seeds, toasted
   (see page 126), or ½ teaspoon ground
¼ teaspoon crushed red pepper flakes
½ cup dry white wine
2 cups fresh sweet corn kernels,
   cut from the cob (about 2 ears)

1 cup husked and diced tomatillos
½ cup diced bell pepper, preferably a mix of red and yellow
4 ounces green beans, ends trimmed, diced
1 medium yellow squash, diced
½ cup freshly grated Parmesan or Asiago cheese,
   plus additional cheese for serving
¼ cup chopped fresh cilantro leaves,
   plus whole sprigs for garnish
Kosher salt and freshly ground black pepper
Carrot-Corn Broth (recipe follows)

1. Bring the vegetable broth to a simmer over medium heat. Reduce the heat to low and keep warm until needed.

2. Heat the olive oil in a large saucepan over medium heat. Add the onion and garlic and cook until soft but not brown, about 5 minutes. Add the barley and cook, stirring often, until the barley is slightly opaque, about 3 minutes.

3. Add the cumin seeds and pepper flakes, then add the wine and cook until all the liquid is absorbed.

4. Add the hot broth, ½ cup at a time, stirring after each addition and cooking until the liquid is almost absorbed.

5. When the barley is nearly tender, add the corn, tomatillos, bell pepper, green beans, and squash. Continue stirring, adding any remaining broth until the vegetables are tender and the barley is creamy but not mushy. Stir in the cheese and cilantro; adjust the seasoning with salt and pepper.

6. To serve, divide the risotto among warmed soup bowls and ladle the carrot-corn broth around. Top each with a sprig of cilantro and serve immediately, with extra cheese on the side.

recipe continues

CARROT-CORN BROTH

4 cups fresh sweet corn kernels (4 large ears)
12 ounces carrots, peeled and roughly chopped
   (about 3 medium carrots)
Vegetable broth, as needed
1½ tablespoons unsalted butter, softened
Tabasco sauce, to taste
Kosher salt and freshly ground black pepper

makes about 2 cups

1. In a blender or juicer, purée the corn and carrots, adding a little vegetable broth as needed to obtain a smooth consistency.

2. Strain the juices into a saucepan and set over medium heat until hot but not simmering. Whisk in the butter, drops of Tabasco sauce, and salt and pepper to taste. Serve warm.

How to Toast Spices and Nuts

Toasting spices and nuts for a few minutes brings out their aromas and intensifies their flavors. A toaster oven or a small sauté pan can be used. Simply place the spices or nuts (one variety at a time) on a foil-covered tray in a toaster oven that has been preheated to 300°F or in a dry pan over medium heat. Stir occasionally to prevent burning. After a couple minutes, the spices or nuts will become fragrant and slightly darker. At this point, remove them from the heat and proceed with the recipe.

SEARED WHITEFISH WITH SWEET CORN, KOHLRABI, AND TOMATO COMPOTE

serves four

With an appealing assortment of textures and flavors, this simple yet unexpected whitefish preparation will enhance any evening. In case you're not familiar with kohlrabi, it's part cabbage, part root; looks like a small, light green (or sometimes purple) turnip; and tastes like a cross between celery root and broccoli stem. This dish is flexible enough that you can substitute any mild fish, such as halibut, red snapper, or John Dory, or swap the kohlrabi for broccoli or cauliflower.

2 tablespoons plus 1 teaspoon extra-virgin olive oil

4 shallots, sliced

4 garlic cloves, sliced

8 plum tomatoes, seeded and diced

Kosher salt and freshly ground black pepper

Sugar to taste

1/4 cup chopped fresh basil leaves

2 tablespoons chopped fresh thyme leaves

4 small kohlrabi, leaves removed

4 (6- to 8-ounce) boneless and skinless whitefish fillets

2 teaspoons grapeseed oil

2 ears white or yellow corn, kernels cut from the cob (about 1 cup), cobs reserved

1. Prepare the compote: In a medium saucepan, heat 2 tablespoons of the olive oil over medium heat and add the shallots and garlic. Cover and cook the mixture until it is soft. Add the tomatoes, reduce the heat, and continue cooking uncovered until thickened. Season to taste with salt, pepper, and sugar. Stir in the chopped basil and thyme. The compote will be thick, like tomato jam.

2. Bring a medium saucepan of salted water to a boil. Meanwhile, with a vegetable peeler, peel off the skin of the kohlrabi and discard; cut each kohlrabi into 1/2-inch wedges. Cook in the boiling water until the tip of a knife pierces through easily, about 10 minutes. Drain and set aside.

3. Preheat the oven to 350°F.

4. Pat the whitefish fillets dry and season generously with salt and pepper. In a large ovenproof skillet, heat the grapeseed oil over medium-high heat until almost smoking. Add the fish and cook on both sides until nicely browned, about 4 minutes per side. If necessary to finish cooking the fish, transfer the skillet to the oven for about 5 minutes, or until the fish is slightly firm to the touch.

5. While the fish is cooking, heat the remaining teaspoon of olive oil in a small sauté pan and cook the kohlrabi and corn to heat through, seasoning to taste with salt and pepper.

6. Place the vegetables in the middle of warmed serving plates. Transfer the whitefish from the oven to the center of each plate, spoon a little compote over each fillet, and serve.

ROASTED HALIBUT WITH FENNEL-TOMATO SAUCE

serves eight

This dish satisfies a protein craving without leaving you lethargic, even on the steamiest night. Don't be deterred by the long list of ingredients. Once they have been assembled, they can be left simmering on the stove while you relax or prepare the rest of the meal. Toasting the spices for a few minutes in a dry pan over medium heat will intensify their flavors. The result is an alluring light sauce that complements any white-fleshed fish.

¼ cup extra-virgin olive oil, plus a small amount for cooking the fish
1 medium yellow onion, sliced
3 stalks celery, chopped
2 medium leeks, chopped
8 garlic cloves, minced
1 small fennel bulb with greens, chopped
4 pounds ripe plum tomatoes (about 14), seeded and chopped
1 tablespoon fennel seeds, toasted (see page 126)
1 tablespoon mustard seeds, toasted (see page 126)
2 bay leaves
Pinch of red pepper flakes
3 star anise, optional
2 cups dry white wine
2 cups low-sodium chicken or vegetable broth
Kosher salt and freshly ground black pepper
8 (6- to 8-ounce) skinless halibut fillets (preferably thick)
8 tablespoons (1 stick) unsalted butter, chilled and cut into small cubes

1. Prepare the fennel-tomato sauce: In a large saucepan, heat the olive oil over medium heat. Add the onion, celery, leeks, and garlic and cook until softened, about 10 minutes. Add the fennel bulb and greens; sauté until wilted, a few more minutes. Add the tomatoes, fennel seeds, mustard seeds, bay leaves, red pepper flakes, and star anise if desired. Add the wine and enough broth to cover. Bring to a boil, reduce the heat, and simmer uncovered for about 45 minutes, until slightly thickened. Strain through a fine-mesh sieve into another saucepan, season to taste with salt and pepper, and set aside. The sauce can be made up to this point and refrigerated overnight.

recipe continues

2. Preheat the oven to 350°F.

3. Pat the fish dry and season both sides with salt and pepper. In a large ovenproof sauté pan, heat a thin film of olive oil over medium-high heat until very hot. Cook the fish on one side until it is nicely browned, about 4 minutes. Carefully flip the fish over, transfer the pan to the oven, and roast for 4 to 5 more minutes, until the fish is opaque at the thickest part (test with the tip of a knife).

4. Return the sauce to a simmer. Whisk in the cubes of butter, one at a time, until incorporated.

5. Ladle a generous amount of sauce into warmed serving bowls, gently place the fish on top, and serve.

SEARED SALMON WITH ARTICHOKES, SALSIFY, AND SAFFRON BROTH

serves four

For a white-tablecloth luncheon or dinner party, I adore the painterly pastel colors of this delicate, well-balanced dish. Feather light without being flimsy, it features crisp salmon in a vibrant saffron infusion surrounded by artichoke hearts and sliced salsify. If you've never had the chance to taste or cook with salsify, I recommend seeking out this lovely, year-round root. Its thin, dark-skinned stalks have a starchy-sweet quality similar to parsnips. If salsify is not available, you can substitute new potatoes, parsnips, celery root, or turnip. Since fresh artichoke hearts take a considerable amount of time to prepare, I use frozen ones as a shortcut.

2 tablespoons extra-virgin olive oil
1 large shallot, sliced
2 garlic cloves, sliced
1 stalk celery, chopped
1 cup dry white wine
1 quart low-sodium chicken or vegetable broth
1 teaspoon saffron (about 3 pinches)
Kosher salt and freshly ground black pepper
2 stalks salsify
8 ounces frozen artichoke hearts, defrosted
4 (6- to 8-ounce) boneless and skinless salmon fillets
1½ tablespoons grapeseed oil
8 tablespoons (1 stick) unsalted butter, chilled, cut into small cubes
2 plum tomatoes, seeded and finely diced

1. Prepare the saffron broth: In a medium saucepan, heat the olive oil over medium-low heat and add the shallots, garlic, and celery. Cover and cook the mixture until it is soft, stirring occasionally, about 5 minutes. Add the white wine, bring to a boil, then reduce the heat and simmer uncovered until the liquid has almost evaporated, about 10 minutes. Add the chicken broth and saffron and simmer until reduced to 1 cup, about 20 minutes. Strain into a clean pan and adjust the seasoning with salt and pepper as desired. The broth can be made up to this point, cooled, and refrigerated overnight.

recipe continues

2. Prepare the salsify: Scrub the stalks well. Using a vegetable peeler, remove the tough outer skin. Slice on the bias into $\frac{1}{2}$-inch pieces. Cook in boiling salted water until tender. Drain and set aside with the artichokes.

3. Pat the salmon fillets dry and season both sides generously with salt and pepper. In a large, heavy skillet or sauté pan, heat the grapeseed oil over medium-high heat until almost smoking. Add the salmon and cook until nicely browned on both sides, 4 to 5 minutes per side. The fish should be firm but supple to the touch and slightly pink in the center. Transfer the fish to a plate and keep it warm.

4. Return the broth to a simmer over low heat and whisk in the cubes of butter, one at a time, until fully melted. Add the artichokes, salsify, and diced tomatoes and cook until warmed through.

5. Spoon the vegetables onto serving plates and place the salmon on top. Spoon additional broth over the salmon and serve.

GRILLED TURKEY BURGERS

serves four

If you're a fan of turkey burgers, you've probably sampled many different versions, from plain to fancy. This one falls somewhere in the middle, speckled with colorful peppers and enough added fat to keep it juicy. At Shutters, it arrives on a pretzel bun that is baked fresh daily right around the corner, but a sourdough or sturdy whole-grain bun will hold up just as well. Serve the burger with your favorite fixings and accompaniments, or try Basic Aïoli (page 235), Seaside Slaw (page 27), and Sweet Potato Fries (opposite).

1 tablespoon extra-virgin olive oil
$\frac{1}{2}$ red bell pepper, finely diced
$\frac{1}{2}$ green bell pepper, finely diced
$\frac{1}{2}$ medium yellow onion, finely diced
1 small red onion, thinly sliced
2 tablespoons Balsamic Vinaigrette (page 238)
$1\frac{1}{2}$ pounds ground turkey breast
$\frac{1}{2}$ teaspoon kosher salt
$\frac{1}{4}$ teaspoon freshly ground black pepper
4 pretzel or whole-wheat buns

1. Preheat a grill to high heat and oil it well.

2. In a medium saucepan, heat the olive oil and sauté the red and green bell peppers and yellow onion until they are soft. Transfer the mixture to a large bowl and set aside to cool.

3. In the same saucepan, combine the red onion slices with the vinaigrette and cook over medium-low heat until they are very soft and caramelized, about 10 minutes. Set aside.

4. Add the turkey to the sautéed vegetables in the bowl and season with the salt and pepper. Form into 4 patties, each about 1 inch thick.

5. Grill the burgers until they are well marked and cooked through, about 5 minutes per side. Slice the buns in half crosswise and grill or warm them in a toaster oven.

6. To serve, top the burgers with the caramelized red onions and arrange on the buns.

SWEET POTATO FRIES

My quest for the perfect fry has become a bit of an obsession, ending with the following recipe. Trust me on a few tricks, such as the size of the fry (which allows for perfect browning outside and cooking inside), the presoak (which removes the starch and makes the outsides crisp), and the type of oil (peanut yields the best flavor). After that, a generous shake of salt is all that is needed. I justify making them for my family (and polishing them off) by reminding myself that sweet potatoes are one of the best sources of vitamins A and C. If you prefer traditional spuds, turn to the recipe for Cowboy Fries (page 184), my kids' favorite.

3 medium sweet potatoes (about 1 $\frac{1}{2}$ pounds), scrubbed
Peanut or grapeseed oil, for deep frying
Kosher salt

1. Using a large sharp knife, cut the sweet potatoes into $\frac{1}{4}$-inch-thick slices, then cut the slices into $\frac{1}{4}$-inch strips (about 3 inches long). Fill a large bowl with ice water and soak the strips for 30 minutes. Drain them in a colander and pat completely dry on kitchen towels.

2. In a deep fryer or heavy pot, heat 4 inches of oil (4 to 6 cups) over medium-high heat to about 370°F. Line a baking sheet with paper towels. Fry the sweet potato sticks in small batches until golden brown, about 4 minutes. With a slotted spoon, transfer the fries to the baking sheet.

3. Sprinkle with salt and serve immediately, or remove the paper towels and place the fries in a warming drawer or low oven until ready to serve.

ROASTED PEPPER AND CORN SUCCOTASH

This confetti-like side dish is a mainstay in our house because it is about the only vegetal fare I can get the kids to eat. It is a colorful complement to any type of burger, steak, grilled fish, or fried chicken. Serve it warm or at room temperature, or make it a day ahead and chill it (it is even delicious right out of the refrigerator). In some supermarkets, you can find frozen preroasted corn and jarred roasted peppers (see Source Guide), shortcuts that won't diminish the flavor.

4 ears white or yellow corn, husks removed
2 scallions, trimmed
2 tablespoons extra-virgin olive oil
½ red onion, diced small
1 red bell pepper, roasted (see below)

1 green bell pepper, roasted (see below)
Juice of ½ lemon
½ bunch cilantro or chervil, finely chopped
Kosher salt and freshly ground black pepper

1. In a dry, cast-iron skillet over high heat or over a hot grill, char the corn and scallions until they are partially blackened, 8 to 10 minutes. Cut the kernels from the cobs and chop the scallions; reserve them in a medium bowl.

2. In the same skillet, heat the olive oil over medium heat and sauté the red onion until soft and lightly colored, 5 minutes. Add to the corn and scallions.

3. Halve the roasted peppers and remove the cores, seeds, and membranes. Dice the peppers and add to the vegetables along with the lemon juice and cilantro.

4. Season the succotash to taste with salt and pepper, transfer to a serving bowl or plates, and serve.

How to Roast Peppers

Using tongs, place a whole pepper over an open flame, turning occasionally, until the skins are completely charred and black, about 10 minutes. Put the pepper in a small bowl, cover with plastic wrap, and let it cool for 10 minutes. Peel off the charred skin, rinsing with a little water if necessary. The pepper will be soft and blackened in spots. Remove the core and seeds.

BEACH TABLE CHIC

Any of these items—on their own or artfully combined—will give your dining table a quick and stylish beach makeover. To be totally transported to the beach, just add water!

Sand, seashells, starfish, and sand dollars Collect these on your travels and scatter them in the center of the table. Add votive candles for a beachy soirée.

Coral Create a centerpiece with several small pieces of white or red coral or one large one, or use smaller pieces to prop up place cards.

Beach glass and pebbles I love the variegated blues and greens mixed with smooth pebbles around a centerpiece.

Bamboo, rattan, raffia, or straw Whether they adorn your placemats, napkin ties, or breadbasket, these materials will give your table a breezy touch.

Tropical fruits and flowers Use pineapples, mangoes, lychees, orchids, and hibiscus as a centerpiece or to decorate a buffet. They're colorful and smell delicious.

Fish netting and nautical flags Cut a table runner from fish netting and drape it artfully down the center of a table. Small nautical flags are available online and at some home stores. For a clever centerpiece, place them in a flower arrangement or in small potted herb plants.

Small buckets Great for children's parties, personalized pails filled with a shovel, crayons, paper, and other take-home goodies delight small guests.

STRAWBERRY-RHUBARB COBBLER

Rosy pink rhubarb stalks begin to appear on produce shelves in the spring and stay until the end of summer. In the spirit of true cobblers, this not-too-sweet version combines a juicy, bubbly filling with a golden biscuit crust. Chopping the rhubarb diagonally will eliminate any residual stringiness, and I recommend ½-inch pieces so that the rhubarb doesn't turn to mush in the oven. If you prefer, red raspberries work beautifully in place of the strawberries, giving a delightful crimson cast to the dessert. You can assemble this recipe the night before or the morning of, refrigerate it, and then bake it just before serving.

FILLING
1 pound rhubarb (5 to 7 stalks)
⅔ cup sugar
1 tablespoon all-purpose flour
1½ cups strawberries (about 12 ounces),
   hulled and halved

TOPPING
1 cup all-purpose flour
3 tablespoons sugar
1½ teaspoons baking powder
Pinch of kosher salt
4 tablespoons unsalted butter, chilled, cut into small pieces
¼ cup half-and-half, or 2 tablespoons whole milk and
   2 tablespoons heavy cream
Crème fraîche or vanilla ice cream, for serving

1. Preheat the oven to 400°F. Butter an 11 × 7-inch glass or ceramic baking dish.

2. Prepare the filling: Peel the rhubarb with a vegetable peeler, removing the tough parts and strings. Slice the rhubarb on the bias into ½-inch pieces. Toss with the sugar and flour and place in the prepared dish. Bake 8 to 10 minutes, until the rhubarb is juicy and bubbling.

3. Meanwhile, prepare the topping: In a medium bowl, combine the flour, sugar, baking powder, and salt. With your fingers or a pastry cutter, blend in the butter until coarse crumbs are formed. Add the half-and-half, mixing until just combined (the batter will be sticky).

4. Remove the rhubarb from the oven. Do not pour off or reduce the juices; you'll want the topping to absorb every last drop. Distribute the strawberries over the rhubarb, then drop spoonfuls of the topping evenly over the fruit. The fruit needn't be covered entirely; the cobbler batter will puff and spread while baking.

5. Return the cobbler to the oven and bake until the topping is golden and the filling is bubbling underneath, 20 to 25 minutes. Serve warm with crème fraîche or vanilla ice cream on the side.

YOGURT MOUSSE WITH HONEY-POACHED APRICOTS

serves six

This exceptionally refreshing dessert is a leap above frozen yogurt, with a similar palate-cleansing tang. I love slathering any leftover poached apricots on bread the next morning.

MOUSSE
2 cups plain whole-milk yogurt
1 $\frac{1}{4}$ cups heavy cream
1 packet unflavored gelatin
1 cup confectioners' sugar

APRICOTS
3 tablespoons honey
$\frac{1}{4}$ cup sugar
$\frac{1}{2}$ vanilla bean, halved lengthwise
6 ounces dried apricots

1. Place a fine-mesh sieve over a small bowl and scoop the yogurt into the sieve. Refrigerate for 30 minutes to drain the yogurt of excess moisture. Measure out 1 cup of yogurt into a small bowl and whisk until smooth.

2. In a small saucepan, combine $\frac{1}{4}$ cup of the cream and the gelatin and let sit for 5 minutes. Gently heat to dissolve the gelatin, about 5 minutes. Gradually whisk the mixture into the yogurt.

3. In a separate bowl, whisk the remaining cup of cream until it holds thick peaks. Whisk in the confectioners' sugar. Fold the whipped cream into the yogurt mixture and pour that into 6 individual ramekins or martini glasses.

4. Freeze the mousses until firm (at least 2 hours or overnight). An hour before serving, transfer them to the refrigerator.

5. Meanwhile, prepare the apricots: In a heavy saucepan, combine the honey, sugar, and vanilla bean with 1 cup water and bring to a simmer. Add the apricots and simmer over medium-low heat until soft but still intact, about 8 minutes. Cool the apricots in the poaching liquid and reserve, or store in an airtight container in the refrigerator for up to 1 week.

6. To serve, spoon some of the apricots and their liquid on top of each mousse.

LEMON CURD WITH FRESH BLACKBERRIES

makes 2 cups lemon curd; serves six to eight

We are a family of dippers. Having a savory or sweet dip for every course is not unusual in our house, where my kids love to dip bread in basil pesto (see page 111), veggies in Louie Dressing (page 243), and fries in Parmesan Dipping Sauce (page 174). This dessert is a welcome way to prolong the fun at the table and keep your guests around well into the night. The lemon curd will keep for 1 week, so you can reach for it any time you need a casual impromptu dessert. You could substitute grapefruit juice or passion fruit purée for the lemon juice and serve store-bought meringue cookies alongside the berries. I like to serve the lemon curd in little espresso cups that I have collected over the years. They don't match but no one ever notices — they're too busy dipping!

1 tablespoon grated lemon zest
1/2 cup fresh lemon juice (from 3 lemons)
1/4 cup fresh Meyer lemon juice (from 1 lemon)
Pinch of kosher salt
8 tablespoons (1 stick) unsalted butter, chilled, cut into pieces
1 1/4 cups sugar
3 large eggs
4 large egg yolks
Fresh blackberries

1. Make the lemon curd: In a heavy saucepan, combine the zest, both kinds of lemon juice, salt, butter, and half of the sugar. Bring to a boil over medium heat.

2. Meanwhile, have ready a fine-mesh strainer set over a medium airtight container and a medium bowl filled halfway with ice water.

3. Whisk together the eggs and yolks in a small bowl. Whisk in the remaining sugar until the egg mixture turns pale, about 2 minutes. Whisking constantly, add a bit of the hot lemon juice mixture to the eggs to temper them, then pour the entire bowl of eggs into the saucepan, whisking vigorously. Lower the heat and continue stirring until the curd has thickened and is bubbling around the edges.

4. Strain the curd into the airtight container, cover the surface with plastic wrap, and set in the bowl of ice water to cool. When fully cooled, store in the refrigerator for up to 1 week.

5. To serve, spoon a little lemon curd into ramekins or small cups and accompany with blackberries and, if desired, a few meringue cookies.

PASSION FRUIT
CRÈME BRÛLÉE

serves six

If creamy desserts are your proclivity, try this lovely fruity custard. Served cold, it delivers just the right amount of tropical sweetness with a velvety texture. Rather than baking the custards in a water bath (which can end up flooding them), I found this stovetop method to be more reliable. If passion fruit purée is not available (see Source Guide), you can make your own fruit purée in the blender using frozen mango or pineapple. You can even skip the brûlée step and serve the custards simply chilled. The desserts will keep individually wrapped in the refrigerator for a few days.

½ cup frozen passion fruit purée, defrosted
2 tablespoons fresh orange juice
1 tablespoon fresh lemon juice
¼ teaspoon vanilla extract
¾ cup sugar, plus more for serving
6 large egg yolks
Pinch of kosher salt
1½ cups heavy cream

1. Combine the passion fruit purée, orange juice, lemon juice, and vanilla in a large bowl. Set a fine-mesh strainer over the bowl and set aside.

2. Combine the sugar, egg yolks, and salt in a medium bowl and whisk until well combined and the mixture turns pale. Whisk in the cream.

3. Transfer the mixture to a medium saucepan. Cook over medium-low heat, stirring constantly and scraping the bottom of the pot with a wooden spoon until slightly thickened, 8 to 12 minutes. Do not let the custard simmer.

4. Pour the custard through the strainer into the bowl with the passion fruit mixture. Stir to combine.

5. Divide the custard evenly among 6 ramekins and allow to cool. Cover with plastic wrap and refrigerate until chilled, at least 4 hours or up to 3 days.

6. To serve, preheat the broiler.

7. Sprinkle a little sugar over the surface of the custards and place them on a baking sheet. Put under the broiler briefly to caramelize the tops, about 1 minute, being careful not to burn the sugar. Serve immediately.

CHOCOLATE MANGO
SEMIFREDDO

serves eight

Semifreddo means "half cold" in Italian, but it doesn't describe half the appeal of this beautifully marbled, mousse-like dessert. It combines the best of mousse and gelato in one, and because it is sliced rather than scooped, it can be eaten with a fork (but I recommend diving in with a spoon). You can serve this luscious dessert either frozen or straight from the refrigerator, and it can be made up to a week ahead of time.

14 ounces semisweet chocolate
Softened butter, for preparing mold
2 large egg whites
2 tablespoons granulated sugar
Pinch of kosher salt
2 cups heavy cream
2 tablespoons confectioners' sugar
6 ounces frozen or fresh mango purée (¾ cup)
2 teaspoons cocoa powder, plus extra for dusting

1. In a double boiler or microwave, melt the chocolate. Let cool to room temperature.

2. Butter a terrine mold or loaf pan and line it with strips of wax paper, draping the edges over the sides of the terrine or pan.

3. Combine the egg whites, granulated sugar, and salt in a bowl, and beat with an electric mixer until the whites form stiff peaks; set aside.

4. In a separate bowl, combine the cream and confectioners' sugar. Whisk by hand or beat with an electric mixer until soft peaks form. Fold the egg whites into the whipped cream.

5. Transfer half of the mixture to a clean bowl. Fold the mango purée into one half and the melted chocolate and cocoa powder into the other.

6. Fill the terrine mold with the two mixtures, alternating and stirring gently to create a marbled effect. Cover with plastic wrap, and refrigerate for at least 6 hours or freeze for at least 3 hours.

7. To unmold the dessert, pull up on the wax paper. Cut the mousse into 1-inch-thick slices and place each slice on a serving plate, dusting it lightly with cocoa powder.

FRESH RASPBERRY SAUCE

makes 1 cup

This intense, ruby red sauce is all you need to dress up a scoop of ice cream or sorbet, or a slice of Lemon Tart (page 95). Drizzled over vanilla bean ice cream (my favorite), it is pure summer lovin'. If you cheat and use frozen raspberries, it'll be our secret. The sauce will stay fresh in the refrigerator for up to 1 week.

1 pint fresh or frozen raspberries
½ cup sugar

In a small saucepan, combine the raspberries, sugar, and 1 cup water over medium heat and bring to a boil. Lower the heat and simmer the sauce until it is slightly thickened, about 10 minutes. Strain the sauce and cool.

SUMMERTIME
ANYTIME PLAYLIST

Just as I like to cook with a variety of flavors, spices, and textures, I mix up my music when having company. Rather than putting together a playlist of Top 40 hits (which everyone has already heard over and over), I try to include selections from lots of different genres and eras, from funk to world beat to jazz to classics. Start out with upbeat songs to set the mood as guests arrive, follow with mellow, ambient music during the meal, and finish the evening with a crescendo of irresistible party tunes. Here are some suggestions to help you put together a frisky surf-and-turf playlist of your own.

Surf's Up

Kick off your evening with songs to put you in a festive beach mood:

"Surf Calypso"—Rudy and the Surf Kings

"Surf Rider"—The Lively Ones

"Summertime Girlfriend"—A.M. Sixty

"Upside Down"—Jack Johnson

"Good Vibrations"—Brian Wilson

"Ocean Avenue"—Yellowcard

"Caravan"—Dick Dale

"Green Onions"—Booker T. and the MGs

"Ghost Rider"—RJD2 remix

Dinner Mix

These classics won't compete with the dinner conversation:

"Beyond the Sea"—Bobby Darin

"Summer Breeze"—Seals and Croft

"Ain't No Mountain High Enough"—Marvin Gaye
    and Tammi Terrell

"Hotel California"—Eagles

"Somewhere Over the Rainbow"—Israel
    Kamakawiwo'ole

"Circle"—Edie Brickell

"Good Riddance (Time of Your Life)"—Green Day

"Slow Like Honey"—Fiona Apple

"Hallelujah"—Jeff Buckley

"Wild Horses"—Charlotte Martin

"Waiting on an Angel"—Ben Harper

"Heartbeat"—Jose Gonzalez

"Woman"—Maroon 5

Life's a Beach

These contemporary rock songs will help you kick up your heels after a good, hearty meal:

"See the World"—Gomez

"Upside Down"—Jack Johnson

"All I Wanna Do"—Sheryl Crow

"Heaven"—Los Lonely Boys

"Even Better Than the Real Thing"—U2

"Sweet Child O' Mine"—Sheryl Crow

"Good Times"—Tommy Lee

"Life Goes On"—John Cougar Mellencamp

"Shower the People"—James Taylor

"Feel Good Inc."—Gorillaz

"Fly Me to the Moon"—Bobby Womack

"Hey Ya!"—Outkast

Turn Up the Heat

No conversation required—these will warm up the room all by themselves:

"Crash"—Dave Matthews Band

"Boys of Summer"—Don Henley

"Each Coming Night"—Iron & Wine

"Your Body's a Wonderland"—John Mayer

"Constant Craving"—K.D. Lang

"Love Song"—311

"Unchained Melody"—Cyndi Lauper

"Wonderful Tonight"—Eric Clapton

"The Way You Look Tonight"—Richard "Cookie" Thomas

"I Wish You Love"—Rachel Yamagata

"In Your Eyes"—Peter Gabriel

"Let's Stay Together"—Al Green

"You and Me"—Lifehouse

"For You I Will"—Teddy Geiger

STORMY NIGHTS

Even in Santa Monica, the occasional storm soaks the beaches and bike paths, turning away disappointed sun-seekers. While hard-charging Angelenos will brave a dreary squall (along with the inevitable traffic) well into the night, I would much rather stay in and hibernate in style. These are the evenings to spend a little more time cooking up comforting meals that may require extra effort but are well worth sharing. I like to enlist some help from my kids or husband for a little kitchen togetherness.

This chapter includes some of Shutters' best heart-warming soups, main dishes, and sides for a blustery evening or even a rainy afternoon. A glamorous Lobster Caesar Salad is all you might need to liven things up, or perhaps the evening calls for a tureen of hearty Wild Mushroom and Leek Soup, followed by Roasted Chicken Breasts with Smoky Lentils and Indoor S'Mores. To plan your menu, mix and match as many dishes as you feel like taking on. Now light the fire and turn up the heat!

STORMYNIGHTS

Butternut Squash Soup with Cinnamon Sticks and Crème Fraîche

Country Chicken Soup

Wild Mushroom and Leek Soup

Radicchio Soup with Smoked Mozzarella Cheese

Roasted Pear Salad with Roquefort Cheese, Walnuts, and Ruby Port Vinaigrette

Gigante Bean Salad with Oven-Dried Tomatoes, Black Olives, and Pesto

Lobster Caesar Salad

Spinach Risotto

Pappardelle with Wild Mushrooms, Rosemary, and Light Tomato Sauce

West Coast Hot Pot

Truffle-Scented Salmon with Mustard Vinaigrette

Roasted Chicken Breasts with Smoky Lentils

Braised Turkey Breast with Wild Mushrooms, Olives, and Oven-Dried Tomatoes

Butcher-Cut Steaks with Parmesan Dipping Sauce

Porcini and Spice-Rubbed Fillet of Beef with Red Wine–Foie Gras Sauce

Grilled Baby Leeks

Roasted Maple-Glazed Spaghetti Squash

Basil Mashed Potatoes and Melted Onions

Steamed Broccoli Rabe with Lemon and Garlic

Cowboy Fries

Celery Root Purée

Creamy Polenta

Apple-Jack Pie with Ginger Custard Sauce

Vanilla Bean and Butterscotch Puddings

Indoor S'Mores

Warm Pineapple Upside-Down Cake

Classic Chocolate Pudding Cakes with Caramel Sauce

BUTTERNUT SQUASH SOUP WITH CINNAMON STICKS AND CRÈME FRAÎCHE

serves six

Gather around the fireplace with mugs of this sweet cinnamon-spiked soup, and the temperature is sure to rise. On special occasions, I add diced roasted chestnuts and a swirl of maple syrup just before serving. Or you can try adding a dash of nutmeg or honey along with the squash. However you make it, this soup exudes coziness on a chilly night.

2 tablespoons unsalted butter
1 medium white onion, chopped
2 carrots, peeled and chopped
2 pounds butternut squash, peeled, seeded, and cut into chunks
About 2 quarts low-sodium chicken or vegetable broth
1 cinnamon stick, plus 6 more for garnish
1 cup heavy cream
Kosher salt and white pepper
Crème fraîche or whipped cream, optional

1. In a large pot over medium heat, melt the butter until it begins to bubble. Add the onion and carrots, cover the pot, and cook until the vegetables are soft, about 10 minutes.

2. Add the squash and continue to cook, uncovered, until heated through, about 5 minutes.

3. Add enough broth to cover the squash by 1 inch, bring to a boil, then lower the heat, drop in the cinnamon stick, and simmer until the squash is completely cooked and soft, about 1 hour.

4. Add the cream, return to a boil for a minute, and adjust the seasoning with salt and pepper to taste. Remove the soup from the heat and let it cool slightly. Discard the cinnamon stick.

5. Working in batches, transfer the soup to a blender and, holding the cover down tightly with a kitchen towel to protect from hot splatters, blend until smooth. If serving immediately, return the soup to the pot and heat until simmering. Alternatively, the soup can be cooled completely and refrigerated for up to 3 days or frozen for 1 month.

6. Serve the soup in mugs, each serving garnished with a dollop of crème fraîche and a cinnamon stick.

COUNTRY CHICKEN SOUP

serves six to eight

There are just about as many variations of recipes for chicken soup as there are shells on a beach. This one is based on the traditional ingredients and garnished at the last minute with freshly cooked vegetables. It couldn't be easier—place all the ingredients in one pot and let the stove do the rest. To make the soup extra flavorful, I employ a little trick learned from some resourceful chefs I met in France: Freeze any broth that is left over and use it to reinforce the next batch. (See photograph, page 151.)

1 whole chicken (about 4 pounds), preferably kosher and organic if available, cut into pieces
2 medium carrots, roughly chopped
2 stalks celery, roughly chopped
2 yellow onions, roughly chopped
½ bunch flat-leaf parsley, washed
4 quarts low-sodium vegetable broth or water, or a combination

Kosher salt
2 tablespoons extra-virgin olive oil
2 medium carrots, peeled and diced into ½-inch cubes
2 stalks celery, sliced into ½-inch pieces
1 medium onion, diced into ½-inch pieces
2 russet potatoes, peeled and diced into ½-inch cubes
1 bunch broccolini, cut into small florets, optional
Large handful of baby spinach

1. To make the soup, combine the chicken, carrots, celery, onions, parsley, and broth in a large pot. Bring to a boil over high heat, then lower the heat and simmer, skimming off the foam and impurities that rise to the surface, until the chicken is cooked, 45 minutes to 1 hour.

2. Remove the chicken from the pot and allow it to cool. Dice the chicken meat, discarding the skin and bones, and set aside. Taste the broth and season with salt if needed.

3. Strain the broth through a large sieve into another pot, discarding the solids. The broth and chicken can be cooled and refrigerated for 1 week. The broth also freezes well for up to 1 month.

4. In a small sauté pan, heat the olive oil and add the carrots, celery, onion, and potatoes; cook until they begin to soften, about 5 minutes. Add the vegetables to the chicken broth and simmer until the potatoes are tender, about 10 minutes.

5. Add the diced chicken meat, broccolini, and spinach to the soup. Simmer until the vegetables are tender, a few minutes. Season with salt to taste and serve piping hot.

WILD MUSHROOM AND LEEK SOUP

serves six

This soup is pure mushroom indulgence. Once puréed, it is so creamy that you could easily omit the cream and never miss it. The earthy meatiness of mushrooms makes this soup substantial enough to stand alongside a salad for an informal dinner, or serve it as an excellent prelude to a hearty second course.

1 tablespoon unsalted butter
1 tablespoon extra-virgin olive oil
1½ pounds mushrooms, washed (see page 26) and chopped
4 large leeks, white and light green parts, roughly chopped
Kosher salt and freshly ground black pepper
Pinch of cayenne pepper
6 cups mushroom broth or low-sodium vegetable broth
1 cup heavy cream, optional
2 tablespoons dry sherry or lemon juice
½ bunch chives, finely chopped

1. In a large soup pot, heat the butter and olive oil over medium-high heat. Add the mushrooms and sauté until they are soft and beginning to brown, about 10 minutes.

2. Add the leeks and cook until soft. Season with salt, pepper, and cayenne pepper, then add the broth. Bring the soup to a boil, then reduce the heat to low, add the cream (if desired) and sherry, and simmer for about 40 minutes, until the flavors have developed.

3. Let the soup cool slightly; then, working in batches if necessary, transfer it to a blender and, covering the lid carefully with a kitchen towel to prevent splattering, blend the soup until smooth.

4. Reheat the soup in the same pot, then ladle into soup bowls and serve piping hot, garnished with the chopped chives.

RADICCHIO SOUP WITH SMOKED MOZZARELLA CHEESE

I must admit the idea of putting radicchio in a soup sounded odd to me, and together with red wine, bread, tomatoes, and cheese, it seemed positively peculiar. But imagine a heady brew of everything you might be craving on a stormy night. The slight bitterness of sautéed radicchio is softened by creamy cubes of smoked cheese, which quickly melt into the soup to give it an intriguing depth that is anything but mundane.

5 tablespoons extra-virgin olive oil
2 medium heads radicchio, cored, quartered, and shredded
Kosher salt and freshly ground black pepper
2 garlic cloves, finely sliced
1 shallot, finely sliced
1 (15-ounce) can diced tomatoes in juice
½ cup hearty red wine
3 cups low-sodium chicken or vegetable broth
4 cups ½-inch-cubed crusty country bread
4 ounces smoked mozzarella or other smoked soft cheese, cut into ¼-inch cubes
¼ cup loosely packed fresh basil leaves, thinly sliced, for garnish

1. In a large, deep saucepan or soup pot over medium-high heat, heat 2 tablespoons of the olive oil. Add the radicchio and cook until it has wilted, about 3 minutes. Season lightly with salt and pepper, then transfer the radicchio to a plate, and set aside.

2. Add 2 more tablespoons of the olive oil to the pan along with the garlic and shallot. Cook until softened but not brown, about 3 minutes. Add the tomatoes, wine, and broth and bring to a boil. Reduce the heat and simmer until the flavors have melded, about 15 minutes. Adjust the seasoning to taste with salt and pepper.

3. Meanwhile, in a small bowl, toss the bread cubes with the remaining tablespoon of olive oil. In a medium sauté pan, toss the bread over medium-high heat until golden brown.

4. To serve, stir the radicchio into the hot soup. Divide the cheese and bread cubes among 6 large soup bowls and ladle the soup over. Garnish with the basil and serve immediately.

ROASTED PEAR SALAD WITH ROQUEFORT CHEESE, WALNUTS, AND RUBY PORT VINAIGRETTE

serves six

You can vary the ingredients in this lusty salad each time you make it by experimenting with different crumbly cheeses, such as goat, Gorgonzola, blue, and Stilton. If you prefer a bacon-free version, a similar smoky flavor can be achieved by substituting a vegetarian bacon product, such as Yves Veggie Canadian Bacon (which you'll need to sauté in a little olive oil since, like most soy substitutes, it does not have its own fat to cook in).

3 Bosc pears, cut into ½-inch wedges
½ cup plus 1 tablespoon extra-virgin olive oil
Kosher salt and freshly ground black pepper
1 tablespoon honey
8 ounces bacon, optional
1 cup ruby port

1 shallot, sliced
1½ tablespoons red wine vinegar
12 cups mixed baby greens
3 ounces Roquefort cheese, crumbled (¾ cup)
1 cup walnut halves, toasted (see page 126)

1. Preheat the oven to 375°F.

2. Toss the pears with 1 tablespoon of the olive oil and season them with salt and pepper. Arrange the pears on a baking sheet and roast them until they are brown in spots, about 20 minutes. Transfer the pears to a small bowl and toss them gently with the honey.

3. In a medium nonstick skillet, cook the bacon (if using) over medium-high heat until crisp and brown, about 5 minutes. Using a slotted spoon, transfer the bacon to paper towels and pat with another paper towel to absorb excess grease. Coarsely chop the bacon.

4. In a medium saucepan, bring the port and shallots to a boil. Reduce the heat to medium-low and simmer until the liquid has reduced to ½ cup, about 8 minutes. Strain the mixture into a medium bowl and let cool.

5. Whisk the vinegar into the reduced port, then whisk in the remaining ½ cup oil in a slow stream. Season with salt and pepper to taste.

6. In a large bowl, lightly toss the greens, cheese, walnuts, bacon, and pears with the dressing. Transfer to a serving bowl or plates and serve immediately.

GIGANTE BEAN SALAD WITH OVEN-DRIED TOMATOES, BLACK OLIVES, AND PESTO

serves six as a first course

Gigante beans, or butter beans, are those giant white beans that you may have eaten once on a trip to France, Greece, or the United Kingdom. Meaty and flavorful, these jumbo-sized lima beans will delight your guests. Toss them with oven-dried tomatoes, a perky black olive dressing, and basil pesto for a multilayered first course that's sure to please.

3 loosely packed cups frisée leaves or watercress sprigs
2 (15-ounce) cans gigante beans, butter beans, or other giant white beans, rinsed and drained
1½ cups Oven-Dried Tomatoes (page 244)
Black Olive Dressing (recipe follows)
½ cup basil pesto (see page 111)
1 tablespoon balsamic vinegar
Kosher salt and freshly ground black pepper

Arrange the frisée in the middle of a serving bowl or 6 plates. Top with the beans and tomatoes. Drizzle the black olive dressing over the salad along with a little basil pesto. Finally, drizzle the balsamic vinegar around, season with salt and pepper, and serve immediately.

BLACK OLIVE DRESSING

½ cup extra-virgin olive oil
3 tablespoons seeded and diced tomato
3 tablespoons finely diced black olives, such as niçoise or kalamata
2 teaspoons grated lemon zest
Kosher salt and freshly ground black pepper

makes about ¾ cup

In a small bowl, whisk together the oil, tomato, olives, and lemon zest and season with salt and pepper. Set aside to marinate for at least 2 hours or refrigerate, covered, for up to 3 days. Bring to room temperature before serving.

LOBSTER
CAESAR SALAD

When a storm keeps you indoors, try putting a little glamour on the plate. With the crispest of romaine leaves, garlic-kissed croutons, and the thrill of tender, decadent lobster chunks, this salad definitely fits the bill. Top it off with a crown of julienned celery root and salmon caviar for an enlivening one-dish meal.

2 (1½-pound) precooked lobsters
2 large hearts of romaine lettuce, leaves separated and roughly chopped
Eggless Caesar Dressing (page 242)
1 small celery root, peeled and cut into thin matchsticks
Garlic Croutons (recipe follows)
¼ cup Parmesan cheese shavings
Salmon caviar, to garnish
Chervil sprigs, to garnish

1. Carefully remove the lobster meat from the shells, cutting the tail meat into 1½-inch chunks and reserving the claw and knuckle portions; set aside.

2. Toss the romaine leaves with a little Caesar dressing and arrange on serving plates.

3. Toss the celery root lightly with additional dressing and arrange it on top of the romaine.

4. Arrange the lobster meat attractively around the salads with the claw meat at the top. Scatter the salads with garlic croutons and shaved Parmesan. Garnish with salmon caviar and chervil.

recipe continues

GARLIC CROUTONS

⅓ cup olive oil
2 large garlic cloves, lightly crushed
2 cups ½-inch bread cubes
2 tablespoons finely minced fresh flat-leaf parsley
1 teaspoon grated lemon zest
Kosher salt and freshly ground black pepper

makes 2 cups

1. Preheat the oven to 375°F.

2. In a small sauté pan, heat the oil over medium heat. Add the garlic and cook it until it is just beginning to color, being careful the garlic doesn't burn (or it will become bitter). Remove the garlic and discard.

3. Toss the bread cubes with the oil and scatter on a baking sheet. Bake until the croutons are golden, turning halfway through, about 20 minutes. Remove from the oven and drain the croutons on paper towels. While still warm, toss the croutons with the parsley, lemon zest, and salt and pepper to taste. Set aside or cool and store in an airtight container for up to 5 days.

SPINACH RISOTTO

serves eight as a side dish or six as a main course

For a quick family dinner, this emerald-colored risotto can be an elegant one-dish meal. For dinner parties, I like to serve it under a simple seared or roasted fish, such as Roasted Halibut with Tomato-Juniper Compote (page 78) or Truffle-Scented Salmon (page 168). To prepare it in advance, simply stop the cooking before the rice is tender, spread the risotto onto a baking sheet to cool, and keep it refrigerated until just before serving time. At the last minute, transfer it back to a pot and add a few more cups of hot broth to finish the cooking. To dress up this festive risotto, you can add chopped porcini or other dried mushrooms that have been reconstituted in hot water. And make sure to pass the Parmesan!

1 pound spinach leaves, stemmed	1 pound Arborio or Carnaroli rice
1 quart low-sodium chicken or vegetable broth	¼ cup dry white wine
3 tablespoons unsalted butter	3 tablespoons mascarpone cheese
1 tablespoon extra-virgin olive oil	½ cup grated Parmesan cheese, plus additional for serving
2 medium shallots, finely minced (about ⅓ cup)	Kosher salt and freshly ground black pepper

1. Bring a large pot of salted water to a boil. Fill a medium bowl halfway with ice water. Add the spinach to the pot and boil it for 1 minute. Drain, then cool in the ice water. Drain the spinach again, leaving a few remaining drops on the leaves to facilitate blending. In a food processor, purée the spinach until it is very smooth; set aside.

2. In a medium saucepan, bring the broth to a boil, and then reduce the heat to very low.

3. Meanwhile, in a medium pot, melt 1 tablespoon of the butter and the olive oil over medium heat. Add the shallots and cook, stirring, until translucent, being careful not to burn them, about 3 minutes. Add the rice and continue to cook and stir until the rice is evenly coated in oil, 1 to 2 minutes. Add the wine and simmer until it has completely evaporated.

4. Begin adding the broth ½ cup at a time, stirring after each addition and cooking until the broth has been absorbed. Continue adding broth and cooking until the rice is tender but al dente (a little firm to the bite). The risotto should bubble gently throughout the cooking process and will be creamy and loose when finished.

5. Stir in the reserved spinach purée, the remaining 2 tablespoons butter, the mascarpone, and the Parmesan cheese; cook briefly to warm through. Season with salt and pepper and serve immediately with additional Parmesan on the side.

PAPPARDELLE WITH WILD MUSHROOMS, ROSEMARY, AND LIGHT TOMATO SAUCE

serves eight as a side dish or four as a main course

Pasta is a weeknight staple in our house, though I must confess I do not have the time to make it from scratch. But I discovered at the local cheese shop several brands of dried fresh pasta (Antonio Marella, Rustichetta d'Abruzzo; see Source Guide) that have taken our favorite mainstay to new heights. Pappardelle is usually hand-cut because of its zigzag edges; it is especially suited to this recipe, in which the soft ribbons are bathed in a savory, satisfying tomato sauce lightened with broth and a touch of cream.

2 tablespoons extra-virgin olive oil

1 large shallot, minced

2 garlic cloves, minced

½ cup dry white wine

10 ripe plum tomatoes, peeled, seeded, and roughly
  chopped, or 1 (15-ounce) can diced tomatoes with juice

1 teaspoon chopped fresh rosemary

½ cup low-sodium chicken or vegetable broth

¼ cup heavy cream or half-and-half, optional

Kosher salt and freshly ground black pepper

1 pound homemade or store-bought pappardelle
  (or other wide pasta)

1 pound assorted wild mushrooms, washed
  (see page 26)

Grated Parmesan cheese, for serving

1. In a large saucepan, heat 1 tablespoon of the oil over low heat and sauté the shallot and garlic until fragrant and translucent, about 3 minutes. Add the white wine, increase the heat to medium, and simmer until the wine has reduced by three-quarters, about 5 minutes. Add the tomatoes and rosemary and continue cooking until the sauce has thickened, about 15 minutes. Add the broth and cook until thickened slightly, about 10 more minutes. Stir in the cream, if desired; simmer for one more minute, and season with salt and pepper.

2. Meanwhile, bring a large pot of salted water to a boil.

3. Transfer the sauce to a blender and, carefully holding a towel over the lid to prevent splattering, blend the sauce; keep warm.

4. Cook the pasta in the boiling water until it is tender but still al dente; drain (do not rinse) it and set aside.

5. While the pasta is cooking, heat the remaining tablespoon of oil in a large skillet over high heat and sauté the mushrooms until they are golden brown, stirring occasionally, about 10 minutes. Season them lightly with salt and pepper.

6. Add the tomato sauce and pasta to the skillet, tossing to blend. With a large serving fork, twirl the pasta and transfer it to serving bowls. Top each portion with extra sauce and grated Parmesan cheese.

WEST COAST
HOT POT

serves six

This is Shutters' version of shellfish chowder, with a few signature touches. First, we keep it on the light side — the clams and mussels bathe in a fragrant, miso-thickened broth. Next, we serve a portion of the seafood whole, so you have to roll up your sleeves to scoop the juicy mollusks from their shells. Finally, we serve our chowder in a lovely covered ceramic pot to preserve the delicious aroma. After all, presentation is everything here in L.A.

1 pound clams (see Note)
1 pound mussels
1 (750-ml) bottle dry white wine
½ cup light or white miso paste
1 tablespoon extra-virgin olive oil
3 strips bacon, diced
2 stalks celery, diced

½ medium yellow onion, diced
2 large russet or Yukon gold potatoes, peeled and diced
1 bay leaf
1 sprig fresh rosemary
1 sprig fresh tarragon
Kosher salt and white pepper
1 cup half-and-half

1. Scrub the clams and mussels well and rinse them thoroughly, removing the beards and discarding any that are already open. In a large pot, bring the wine and 2 cups of water to a simmer over medium heat. Add the shellfish, cover, and steam just until the shells open up, 4 to 6 minutes.

2. Remove the shellfish from the broth and discard any unopened shells. Loosen half the clams and mussels from their shells and chop them, keeping the other half in their shells.

3. Strain the broth into a large bowl through a fine-mesh sieve lined with a coffee filter or cheesecloth. Gradually whisk the miso paste into the broth until it has dissolved. Reserve the broth along with the shellfish.

4. In the same pot, heat the olive oil over medium heat. Cook the bacon, celery, and onion until the vegetables are translucent, about 5 minutes. Add the chopped clams and mussels, potatoes, reserved broth, bay leaf, rosemary, and tarragon. Simmer for 20 minutes or until the potatoes are tender. Season to taste with salt and pepper.

5. Add the whole mussels and clams in their shells and the half-and-half, and simmer until heated through, 1 to 2 minutes. Remove the herb sprigs, transfer the soup to a covered ceramic crock or serving dish, and serve immediately.

NOTE
Before putting fresh clams and mussels into the refrigerator, open up the paper they're wrapped in to allow them to breathe. This will prevent the shells from opening prematurely.

TRUFFLE-SCENTED
SALMON WITH
MUSTARD VINAIGRETTE

serves six

The key ingredient for this luxurious recipe is black or white truffle oil, a delicacy that can be found in most gourmet shops and high-end supermarkets. Use it sparingly just before serving — a couple drops will impart plenty of flavorful aroma, and a small bottle will last you just short of a lifetime. I like to pair this simple pan-seared salmon with Spinach Risotto (page 163) or a large bowl of Cowboy Fries (page 184).

1 cup low-sodium chicken or mushroom broth
2 tablespoons Dijon mustard
$\frac{1}{4}$ cup sherry vinegar
1 medium shallot, roughly chopped
$\frac{1}{4}$ cup plus 1 tablespoon grapeseed oil
Kosher salt and freshly ground black pepper
6 (6-ounce) boneless, skinless salmon fillets
Black or white truffle oil
1 small bunch chives, finely chopped

1. Prepare the mustard vinaigrette: Heat the broth to just below a simmer. Pour it into a blender, add the mustard, vinegar, and shallot, and blend until smooth. With the motor running, slowly add the $\frac{1}{4}$ cup grapeseed oil and blend until emulsified. Adjust the seasoning to taste.

2. Pat the salmon fillets dry and season both sides generously with salt and pepper. In a large, heavy skillet or sauté pan, heat the remaining 1 tablespoon grapeseed oil over medium-high heat until almost smoking. Add the salmon and cook without disturbing until nicely browned on both sides, about 4 minutes per side. The fish should be firm but supple to the touch and slightly pink in the center. Transfer the fish to a plate and keep warm.

3. Spoon a little vinaigrette in the center of each warmed serving plate. Place the fish on top and dot it with a few drops of truffle oil. Sprinkle with the fresh chives and serve.

ROASTED CHICKEN BREASTS
WITH SMOKY LENTILS

Because of their earthy flavor and no-soak ease, lentils are one of my favorite legumes to serve alongside nearly any main dish. Served warm, room temperature, or cold (see Notes), they are an excellent source of low-fat protein, iron, and fiber. As with beans, it is important to season them with salt at the end of the cooking process so that they do not lose their shape. Add roasted chicken breasts, perhaps with a side of Tuscan Kale (page 89), Celery Root Purée (page 185), or Fluffy Couscous (page 122), and you have a substantial meal to weather any storm.

2 strips bacon, finely diced
1 medium yellow onion, finely diced
1 stalk celery, finely diced
1 medium carrot, finely diced
2 cups French or black lentils
5 cups low-sodium chicken or vegetable broth
Kosher salt and freshly ground black pepper
6 (6-ounce) boneless chicken breasts, skin removed if desired
2 teaspoons extra-virgin olive oil
$\frac{1}{4}$ cup dry white wine
$\frac{1}{2}$ bunch chives, chopped

1. In a medium saucepan, cook the bacon over medium heat until the fat is released and the bacon is slightly browned. Add the onion, celery, carrot, and lentils and, stirring to coat them, cook for 2 minutes. Add 4 cups of the broth and enough water to cover the lentils by 1 inch, bring to a boil, then reduce the heat to very low and simmer until the lentils are tender but not falling apart, about 25 minutes. Season to taste with salt and pepper. Drain any excess liquid and keep the lentils warm.

2. Preheat the oven to 400°F.

3. Season the chicken liberally with salt and pepper. In a heavy ovenproof sauté pan over medium-high heat (working in batches if necessary), heat the olive oil until very hot. Add the chicken breasts, skin side down, and cook until golden brown, about 4 minutes. Flip the chicken over and transfer the pan to the oven. Roast the chicken until it is cooked through (a meat thermometer should measure 160°F), about 15 minutes.

recipe continues

4. Remove the chicken breasts to a plate; cover and keep warm. Drain any fat from the pan that the chicken was cooked in, add the wine, and simmer over medium heat until nearly evaporated, 1 to 2 minutes. Add the remaining 1 cup of chicken broth and reduce until thickened. Adjust the seasoning as desired.

5. To serve, spoon some lentils in the center of each serving plate, and then place a chicken breast on top. Spoon the sauce over and around the chicken and sprinkle with the chopped chives. Serve immediately.

NOTES
I like to use smoked salt (see Source Guide) in the lentils to enhance the smokiness of the bacon.

Leftover lentils make a delicious cold salad for picnics or an elegant appetizer. Toss them with Balsamic Vinaigrette (page 238) or Sherry Vinaigrette (page 241), sprinkle with a handful of chopped chives, and present them in a colorful bowl or in radicchio cups, with extra vinaigrette drizzled on top. To dress up the salad even further, top the lentils with a few sautéed scallops, grilled shrimp, or slices of smoked salmon.

BRAISED TURKEY BREAST WITH WILD MUSHROOMS, OLIVES, AND OVEN-DRIED TOMATOES

serves six to eight

A modern riff on coq au vin, this is a wonderful special-occasion dish to serve either individually plated or family-style. Instead of turkey, you can substitute chicken, duck, quail, or squab (cooking times will vary). As with any recipe that involves braising, be sure to take the time to brown the meat well to enhance the flavor of the sauce and add rich color to the dish. Serve on a bed of Creamy Polenta (page 186), Fluffy Couscous (page 122), or Basil Mashed Potatoes (page 182) to soak up the hearty juices.

TURKEY

1 half turkey breast (3 to 4 pounds)
Kosher salt and freshly ground black pepper
All-purpose flour, for dusting
2 tablespoons extra-virgin olive oil
1 large yellow onion, chopped
1 medium carrot, chopped
1 stalk celery, chopped
2 garlic cloves, minced
2 cups chopped fresh or canned diced tomatoes in juice
1 tablespoon chopped fresh rosemary leaves
1 tablespoon fresh thyme leaves or 2 teaspoons dried
1 teaspoon whole fennel seeds
$1\frac{1}{2}$ cups hearty red wine
4 cups low-sodium chicken or vegetable broth

MUSHROOMS

$\frac{1}{2}$ ounce dried porcini mushrooms
2 tablespoons extra-virgin olive oil
1 medium shallot, minced
12 ounces assorted wild mushrooms, such as chanterelle, oyster, and shiitake, washed (see page 26), and sliced
8 pieces Oven-Dried Tomatoes (page 244), diced
$\frac{1}{2}$ cup pitted, sliced kalamata or niçoise olives
1 teaspoon grated lemon zest
Kosher salt and freshly ground black pepper

1. Preheat the oven to 350°F.

2. Season the turkey liberally with salt and pepper. Dust with flour, shaking off any excess. Heat the olive oil in a large ovenproof pot with a cover over medium-high heat and brown the turkey on all sides. Remove the turkey from the pot and set aside. Lower the heat to medium.

3. Add the onion, carrot, celery, and garlic to the pot and cook until just beginning to brown, about 10 minutes. Add the tomatoes, rosemary, thyme, fennel seeds, wine, and broth and bring to a boil.

4. Return the turkey to the pot, cover, and braise in the oven for 50 to 60 minutes, until the meat is very tender and falling off the bone.

5. Meanwhile, put the porcini in a small bowl and cover with hot water. Let soak until softened, about 15 minutes. Drain, rinse, and drain again. Chop finely and reserve.

6. Remove the turkey and strain the braising liquid into a medium saucepan, discarding the vegetables. Skin and bone the turkey and separate the meat into pieces, then cover with foil and set aside to keep warm. Boil the braising liquid over high heat until reduced by at least half, or until lightly thickened, 10 to 12 minutes. Season to taste with salt and pepper and keep warm.

7. While the braising liquid is reducing, prepare the mushrooms: Heat the olive oil over medium-high heat in a large skillet and cook the porcini mushrooms and shallot until just beginning to color. Add the fresh mushrooms and cook until well browned, about 10 minutes. Stir in the tomatoes, olives, and lemon zest and season to taste with salt and pepper. Set aside and keep warm.

8. To serve, arrange the turkey pieces in shallow bowls and top with the mushroom mixture. Ladle plenty of sauce over and serve immediately.

BUTCHER-CUT STEAKS WITH PARMESAN DIPPING SAUCE

serves four

On those nights when only a good old-fashioned steak will do, here is the perfect recipe. A Parmesan dipping sauce takes the steaks well beyond the realm of the ordinary. Serve them with Cowboy Fries (page 184), and leftovers are quite unlikely. By the way, the sauce is also delicious with a thick piece of grilled fish.

2 teaspoons extra-virgin olive oil
2 medium shallots, minced
1 garlic clove, minced
$\frac{1}{4}$ cup dry white wine
1 cup heavy cream, plus extra if needed
1 cup freshly grated Parmesan cheese
4 ounces Fontina cheese, grated (1 cup)
4 (6- to 8-ounce) steaks (filet mignon, strip, New York, or other desired cut),
    preferably each 1$\frac{1}{2}$ inches thick
Kosher salt and freshly ground black pepper

1. Prepare the Parmesan dipping sauce: Heat the olive oil in a medium saucepan over low heat. Add the shallots and garlic and cook, stirring, until fragrant but not brown, about 2 minutes. Add the wine and simmer until nearly evaporated, 1 to 2 minutes. Add the cream, increase the heat to medium, and simmer until slightly thickened. Remove the sauce from the heat and whisk in the cheeses. Thin with a little extra cream if needed. Blend the sauce in a blender if a smoother sauce is desired; keep warm.

2. Preheat a grill to high heat or preheat the broiler. When hot, oil the grill well.

3. Season the steaks generously with salt and pepper. Grill or broil until nicely marked or browned on one side, 3 to 5 minutes (the time will vary according to the cut of steak). Turn the steaks over and continue cooking them to desired doneness, 2 to 4 more minutes for medium-rare or 4 to 6 more minutes for medium. Remove the steaks from the heat and allow them to rest for 5 minutes before serving.

4. Pour the sauce into individual ramekins and serve alongside each steak.

PORCINI AND SPICE-RUBBED FILLET OF BEEF WITH RED WINE–FOIE GRAS SAUCE

serves six to eight

Festive enough to serve a crowd on a holiday or special occasion but simple enough to prepare for a family dinner, this distinguished dish gets its flavors from the unusual spice rub and the velvety red-wine-and-port reduction. One rainy night, to appease my red meat–adverse friends, I tried the porcini rub on some thick fillets of halibut, eliminated the foie gras from the sauce, and instead whisked in a few bits of chilled butter. Either way, the dish will make you look like a professional.

PORCINI SPICE RUB
2 ounces dried porcini mushrooms
2 tablespoons juniper berries
1 tablespoon black peppercorns
1 teaspoon fennel seed
1 teaspoon coriander seed
4 whole cloves

BEEF
1 (4-pound) fillet of beef, trimmed
1 tablespoon extra-virgin olive oil
Kosher salt

RED WINE–FOIE GRAS SAUCE
2 tablespoons extra-virgin olive oil
6 ounces cremini or shiitake mushrooms, washed (see page 26) and chopped
2 garlic cloves, minced
2 large shallots, chopped
1 quart low-sodium beef broth
2 cups hearty red wine
1 cup ruby port
4 ounces foie gras or unsalted butter (1 stick), chilled and diced
Kosher salt and freshly ground black pepper

1. Using a spice or coffee bean grinder, grind the porcini, juniper berries, peppercorns, fennel seed, coriander seed, and cloves to a coarse powder.

2. Rub the beef with the oil and then season it generously with salt. Rub in the porcini spice powder. Cover the meat with plastic wrap and set aside for at least 30 minutes or refrigerate overnight.

3. Preheat the oven to 500°F. Allow the meat to come to room temperature.

4. Over a medium-high flame, heat an ovenproof pan large enough to accommodate the beef. Add the olive oil and, when it is almost smoking, add the meat and brown well on all sides.

5. Transfer the pan to the oven and roast the meat for 20 to 30 minutes or until it reaches an internal temperature of 120°F to 125°F for rare, or until it is slightly soft to the touch. Transfer the meat to a cutting board, cover it tightly with foil, and allow it to rest for at least 20 minutes.

6. In the meantime, prepare the sauce: Heat the olive oil in a deep saucepan and cook the mushrooms, garlic, and shallots until lightly browned, about 10 minutes. Add the broth, wine, and port and boil over high heat until reduced by half, approximately 15 minutes. Strain into a clean pan and return to medium heat, simmering until it thickens. You should end up with about 2 cups of sauce. Just before serving, whisk in the foie gras and adjust the seasoning with salt and pepper.

7. To serve: Slice the meat into thick rounds and arrange them on warmed serving plates. Spoon the sauce around and serve immediately.

TEN WAYS TO DECORATE
A GLASS HURRICANE

A simple glass hurricane fitted with a neutral-colored candle (my favorite is chocolate brown) can be cleverly transformed for a stroke of beach chic. Try accessorizing it with any of the following:

1 Sand, seashells, and baby starfish from your favorite beach vacation

2 Sea urchins of all colors and sizes

3 White or pink coral

4 Smooth stones, beach glass, or marbles

5 Orchid or hibiscus blossoms, or petals from your favorite flowers

6 Water and real fish

7 Water tinted with blue food coloring

8 A bamboo or rattan placemat wrapped around the outside and tied with raffia

9 Coarse sea salt (tint it with your favorite food coloring)

10 Plastic pearl beads (available by the roll online)

GRILLED
BABY LEEKS

If you cannot find the early-spring baby leeks, grown-up leeks are also delicious grilled, but they need to be boiled or steamed first to hasten the cooking. You can also substitute spring onions or scallions. Try serving them with Basic Aïoli (page 235) or your favorite vinaigrette for a lovely first course.

1¼ pounds baby leeks, dark green leaves and roots trimmed
¼ cup extra-virgin olive oil
Kosher salt and freshly ground black pepper

1. Preheat the grill to medium-high. Cut the leeks in half lengthwise and wash them well to remove any dirt; pat dry.

2. Rub each leek half with a little oil and season with salt and pepper. Grill until charred and soft. Serve hot, warm, or at room temperature.

ROASTED MAPLE-GLAZED SPAGHETTI SQUASH

serves six

I like to serve this vitamin-packed winter squash with any main dish that either has a tinge of sweetness, such as roasted salmon, or needs a splash of color, like grilled steak or chicken breasts.

1 large spaghetti squash (about 4 pounds)
Kosher salt and freshly ground black pepper
½ cup maple syrup

1. Preheat the oven to 350°F. Line a backing sheet with foil.

2. Slice the squash in half lengthwise. Remove the seeds and season the flesh liberally with salt, pepper, and maple syrup. Place on the baking sheet cut side up.

3. Roast the squash until tender, about 25 minutes.

4. Remove the squash from the oven, reserving any cooking juices. When it is cool enough to handle, use a fork to separate the squash into strands. Transfer to a serving bowl, pour in the reserved juices, and adjust the seasoning if necessary with additional salt and pepper.

BASIL
MASHED POTATOES
AND MELTED ONIONS

serves six

Onions and potatoes are always in stock at my house. If they are at yours, you can easily whip up this earthy side dish to accompany just about any roasted or grilled fish, poultry, or meat. If fresh basil is not in season, substitute a handful of fresh spinach leaves, which will give the same appealing green tint to the fluffy potato purée. (See photograph, page 86).

6 tablespoons (¾ stick) unsalted butter, softened
2 medium yellow onions, thinly sliced
1 cup low-sodium chicken or vegetable broth
Kosher salt and freshly ground black pepper
1 bunch fresh basil, leaves only, plus a few whole sprigs for garnish
2½ pounds russet potatoes (about 4 large), peeled but left whole
1 cup buttermilk or whole milk

1. In a large skillet, heat 3 tablespoons of the butter over medium heat and cook the onions, stirring occasionally, until they begin to brown, about 10 minutes. Add the broth and braise the onions, uncovered, over low heat until they are very soft, about 30 minutes, adding water periodically as needed to prevent burning. Season with salt and pepper to taste and keep warm.

2. Bring a large pot of salted water to a boil. Fill a medium bowl halfway with ice water. Add the basil leaves to the pot and blanch for 1 minute. Transfer them with a slotted spoon to the bowl of ice water (reserve the pot of boiling water). Once cool, drain the basil, chop it roughly, and purée in a blender, adding a little cold water as needed to make a thick purée; reserve.

3. In the same pot of boiling water, cook the potatoes until they are very soft, about 25 minutes.

4. Meanwhile, in a small pot or in the microwave, heat the buttermilk until hot but not boiling. Turn off the heat, cover the pot, and keep warm.

5. Drain the potatoes well. Peel them while they are hot (skewer them on a fork and use a paring knife so that you don't burn yourself) and chop them into chunks. Pass them through a ricer or mash them with a fork in the pot, stirring in the remaining 3 tablespoons butter, then the hot buttermilk, basil purée, and salt and pepper to taste.

6. To serve, spoon the mashed potatoes into a serving bowl or onto plates and top with the onions. Garnish with the fresh basil sprigs.

STEAMED BROCCOLI RABE
WITH LEMON AND GARLIC

serves four

Also known as rapini, broccoli rabe has become a popular side dish in our local Italian restaurants, often replacing its cousin, broccoli. I've adopted it as my current favorite for its bright green color, edible stems, and frisky bite. A little garlic and a dash of hot chile flakes are perfect diversions from its slight bitterness.

8 ounces broccoli rabe, coarse stem ends and yellow leaves removed
3 tablespoons unsalted butter
2 small garlic cloves, minced
2 tablespoons chopped fresh flat-leaf parsley
Pinch of red pepper flakes (optional)
Kosher salt and freshly ground black pepper
2 teaspoons grated lemon zest

1. Bring 1 inch of salted water to a simmer in a medium covered saucepan over medium heat and steam the broccoli rabe until tender but crisp, about 5 minutes. Drain the broccoli rabe well, and dry it on a kitchen towel.

2. In a medium sauté pan, heat the butter over low heat until foaming. Add the garlic and cook slowly until lightly golden, about 2 minutes. Add the broccoli rabe, parsley, red pepper flakes, and salt and pepper to taste. Toss to coat evenly and heat through, a few minutes. Arrange on a serving platter and sprinkle with the lemon zest.

COWBOY
FRIES

Beware of these highly addictive fried spuds — the Parmesan and garlic make them irresistible! Go for broke and serve them with Butcher-Cut Steaks (page 174) or even a refined piece of fish such as Truffle-Scented Salmon with Mustard Vinaigrette (page 168).

2½ pounds russet potatoes (about 4 large), unpeeled
Peanut or canola oil, for frying
¼ cup freshly grated Parmesan cheese
3 garlic cloves, minced
2 tablespoons chopped fresh flat-leaf parsley
Kosher salt and freshly ground black pepper

1. Using a sharp large knife, cut the potatoes into ½-inch slices, and then cut the slices into ½-inch strips (about 3½ inches long). Fill a large bowl with ice water and soak the strips for 30 minutes. Drain them in a colander and pat completely dry on kitchen towels.

2. In a deep fryer or heavy pot, heat 4 inches of oil (4 to 6 cups) over medium-high heat to about 375ºF. Line a baking sheet with paper towels. Fry the potato sticks in small batches until golden brown, about 4 minutes. With a slotted spoon, transfer the fries to the baking sheet to absorb excess oil.

3. In a bowl, toss the fries with the Parmesan cheese, garlic, parsley, and salt and pepper to taste. Serve immediately, or place the fries in a warming drawer or 350ºF oven until ready to serve.

CELERY ROOT
PURÉE

For a simple variation on mashed potatoes, celery root (or celeriac) purée is a stellar accompaniment to any dish with a sauce to sop up, such as Braised Turkey Breast with Wild Mushrooms, Olives, and Oven-Dried Tomatoes (page 172), Porcini and Spice-Rubbed Fillet of Beef with Red Wine–Foie Gras Sauce (page 176), or Roasted Salmon with Grain Mustard and Herbs (page 79).

2 pounds celery root, peeled, trimmed, and cut into large cubes
2 cups milk
Kosher salt
4 tablespoons (½ stick) unsalted butter
White pepper to taste

1. Place the celery root in a medium pot with the milk and enough water to cover. Add a pinch of salt, bring to a boil, then lower the heat and simmer until very soft, about 10 minutes.

2. Drain the celery root, reserving some of the cooking liquid. In a food processor, blend with a little of the cooking liquid to make a smooth, thick purée. Transfer to a bowl, stir in the butter, and season with salt and white pepper to taste. Serve immediately.

CREAMY POLENTA

Long before pasta was invented, there was polenta, the creamy cornmeal porridge that is still a cold-weather staple in Italy. Mixed simply with Parmesan cheese and a little seasoning, this dish is a brilliant accompaniment to any braised or roasted meat or poultry, as it is meant to capture any luscious cooking juices or sauce set upon it. Polenta also makes for a superbly comforting first course or light meal when served in a soup bowl and topped with sautéed mushrooms or basil pesto (see page 111).

1 quart low-sodium chicken or vegetable broth
1⅔ cups polenta or coarse yellow cornmeal
½ cup freshly grated Parmesan or Pecorino cheese
2 tablespoons chopped fresh flat-leaf parsley
Kosher salt and freshly ground black pepper
2 tablespoons unsalted butter, optional

1. In a heavy medium saucepan, bring the broth and 3 cups water to a boil. Add the polenta, whisking constantly and slowly to prevent lumps. Reduce the heat to low and simmer, stirring frequently with a wooden spoon to prevent the polenta from burning, for 25 to 30 minutes, or until the polenta is soft and smooth. Add a little more water if the polenta seems too thick. It should have the consistency of a soft pudding.

2. Stir in the cheese, parsley, and salt and pepper to taste. Stir in the butter, if desired. Serve immediately.

APPLE-JACK PIE
WITH GINGER CUSTARD SAUCE

serves eight

When a storm is at fever pitch, I like to serve this bubbly apple pie to keep everyone's spirits up. As pies go, this one pulls out all the stops, with unexpected surprises like aged Jack cheese, raisins, almonds, and a ginger-scented vanilla sauce.

FILLING

5 cups tart green apples, peeled, cored, and sliced

2 tablespoons fresh lemon juice

½ cup brown sugar, or to taste

2 tablespoons all-purpose flour

¼ teaspoon freshly ground white pepper

2 teaspoons ground cinnamon

½ teaspoon freshly grated nutmeg

⅓ cup golden raisins, soaked in brandy or
   Grand Marnier, if desired, optional

1 unbaked 9-inch piecrust

TOPPING

½ cup granulated sugar

½ cup all-purpose flour

6 tablespoons (¾ stick) unsalted butter, chilled and cut into small bits

3 ounces dry aged Jack cheese, shredded (¾ cup)

¼ cup almonds, toasted (see page 126) and finely chopped

Ginger Custard Sauce (recipe follows; optional)

1. Preheat the oven to 350°F.

2. Prepare the filling: In a large bowl, mix together the apples, lemon juice, brown sugar, flour, white pepper, cinnamon, nutmeg, and raisins. Fill the pie shell evenly with the filling.

3. Prepare the topping: In a food processor, combine the sugar, flour, butter, cheese, and almonds. Pulse the machine a few times to form a coarse, crumbly mixture. Scatter the topping evenly over the filling.

4. Bake the pie until the topping is golden brown and the apples are tender and bubbling, about 45 minutes.

5. Serve hot or at room temperature, with the Ginger Custard Sauce on the side.

recipe continues

GINGER CUSTARD SAUCE

This crème anglaise with a ginger spin can also gussy up an Apple-Cinnamon Crisp (page 92), Warm Pineapple Upside-Down Cake (page 194), or a bowl of fresh peaches or pears. Leftover sauce will keep covered in the refrigerator for up to 5 days.

3 tablespoons roughly chopped fresh ginger
⅓ cup sugar
4 large egg yolks
1½ cups whole milk
1 teaspoon vanilla extract

makes about 2 cups

1. In a small saucepan, simmer the ginger, sugar, and ¼ cup water over medium-low heat for approximately 6 minutes, until the mixture has thickened to a syrup but is not brown. Remove from the heat and let the syrup sit for 30 minutes to infuse; it can also be refrigerated overnight.

2. Meanwhile, in a medium bowl, whisk the egg yolks until slightly thickened; set aside.

3. Fill a medium bowl halfway with ice water and have ready a second bowl that fits inside it.

4. Return the ginger syrup to low heat, add the milk and vanilla, and bring the mixture just to a simmer. Add this mixture very gradually into the beaten yolks, stirring constantly with a whisk to avoid scrambling the eggs.

5. Return the sauce to the pan over medium heat and cook, stirring constantly, until the sauce just begins to thicken, being careful not to let it boil, or it will begin to curdle (the temperature should be about 170°F, and no higher than 180°F).

6. Immediately strain into the smaller bowl, set it into the ice bath, and chill until cold.

VANILLA BEAN
PUDDING

Rewind back to your childhood dessert days and you're sure to fondly remember pudding. This grown-up version gives you reason to relive those luscious memories. Vanilla and butterscotch are always popular at our house, so I like to split the difference and layer dainty teacups or espresso cups with both (see Butterscotch Pudding, below). Either recipe on its own more than satisfies a craving for a creamy, homey dessert.

3 tablespoons cornstarch
½ cup sugar
¼ teaspoon kosher salt
1 cup heavy cream
4 large egg yolks
2 cups whole milk
1 vanilla bean, split lengthwise, or 1 tablespoon vanilla extract

1. Fill a medium bowl halfway with ice water and have ready a fine-mesh strainer set over a medium bowl.

2. Sift the cornstarch, sugar, and salt into a medium heavy-bottomed saucepan. Slowly whisk in the cream, followed by the yolks, milk, and the vanilla bean. Bring the mixture to a simmer over medium-high heat, stirring constantly with a whisk, about 8 minutes. Once it is simmering, reduce the heat to medium and cook the mixture, stirring constantly with a wooden spoon and scraping the bottom and sides of the pot, until it coats the spoon very thickly, 1 to 2 minutes. Be careful not to let the mixture boil, or it will begin to curdle (the temperature should be about 200°F).

3. Immediately pour the pudding through the strainer into the bowl and set it over the ice bath. Discard the vanilla bean. Cover the surface of the pudding with plastic wrap and let it cool completely.

4. Pour into ramekins or teacups and refrigerate for at least 3 hours or overnight. The puddings may be kept, covered, in the refrigerator for up to 3 days.

BUTTERSCOTCH PUDDING >

Follow the recipe for Vanilla Pudding but omit the vanilla bean and add ½ cup butterscotch chips to the thickened cream mixture in step 2. Whisk until the butterscotch chips have melted, and then strain the pudding and proceed with the recipe. Once the puddings have chilled, melt ¾ cup butterscotch chips with 2 tablespoons heavy cream in a small covered bowl in the microwave, stir until smooth, pour over the custard, and serve.

INDOOR
S'MORES

serves two

The ultimate in sweet simplicity, s'mores conjure up delicious memories of campfires and carefree times. You don't even need to build a fire to make this version, which gets an extra jolt of flavor from melted chocolate sprinkled with sea salt, served on the side for shamelessly messy dipping. Somehow the salty beach spin is extra addictive, all the better to savor every bit of deliciously sticky nostalgia!

2 (10-inch) bamboo skewers
3 ounces semisweet chocolate
Pinch of coarse-grained sea salt
2 large marshmallows
4 whole graham crackers

1. Soak the skewers in cold water for 10 minutes to prevent them from burning over the open flame. Drain and dry well.

2. Melt the chocolate carefully in a microwave or over a double boiler to prevent it from burning. Pour into 2 ramekins and sprinkle a few grains of sea salt on top of each.

3. Place a marshmallow on each skewer and heat the marshmallows over an open flame until they begin to brown on the outside and are soft inside.

4. Break the graham crackers in half, sandwich the marshmallows between them, and serve immediately with the melted chocolate on the side for dipping.

WARM PINEAPPLE UPSIDE-DOWN CAKE

makes 6 miniature bundt cakes, or 1 (9-inch) cake to serve eight

A retro dessert turned chic again, these moist and luscious cakes are as pretty to behold as they are delicious. If you don't have mini Bundt cake molds, use large muffin tins or a 9-inch cast-iron skillet. Skip the maraschino cherry garnish (so '70s) and instead go for a puddle of rich Caramel Sauce (page 249) or Ginger Custard Sauce (page 189), perhaps with coconut sorbet and additional chopped pineapple on the side.

Baking spray, for preparing pan
1 cup Caramel Sauce (page 249), plus extra
    for serving, if desired
1 pineapple, sliced into ¼-inch-thick rings
    (reserve scraps to dice and serve on the side)
¾ cup sliced almonds, toasted (see page 126)
    and finely chopped
8 tablespoons (1 stick) unsalted butter, softened
¾ cup sugar

2 large eggs
1 teaspoon vanilla extract
1½ cups all-purpose flour
½ teaspoon kosher salt
1 tablespoon baking powder
¾ teaspoon ground cinnamon
½ cup whole milk

1. Preheat the oven to 350°F. Spray miniature Bundt cake molds with baking spray; set aside.

2. Scoop 2 to 3 tablespoons of caramel in the bottom of each mold and follow with a ring of pineapple for each. (If you are using a skillet, spread the caramel sauce on the bottom and arrange the pineapple rings in a circle around the bottom and sides of the skillet.) Sprinkle with the almonds.

3. In the bowl of an electric mixer, beat together the butter and sugar, scraping the bowl occasionally, until the mixture is light and fluffy. Add the eggs one at a time, beating after each addition. Add the vanilla.

4. In a large bowl, whisk together the flour, salt, baking powder, and cinnamon. Add the butter mixture and milk to the dry ingredients, alternating in thirds, stirring until well combined. Scoop the batter into the molds.

5. Place the cakes on a baking sheet and bake, rotating halfway through, until a toothpick inserted in the middle comes out clean, 30 to 35 minutes. Remove the cakes from the oven and allow to rest for 10 minutes. Carefully invert the cakes onto the baking sheet and then place on serving plates. Serve warm, with additional caramel sauce on the side.

CLASSIC CHOCOLATE PUDDING CAKES WITH CARAMEL SAUCE

serves eight

You could say I have had an affair with this dessert since the night I got married. My wedding was one of the first to happen at our hotel, and I must say it was quite a party. But in the midst of all the hoopla, my husband and I didn't have a minute to eat even a bite of dinner. By the time we got to our newlywed suite in the wee morning hours, we were ravenous. This dessert came to the rescue and has continued to entice me ever since. If there is such a thing as a romantic dessert, this is it!

Baking spray or butter and flour, for preparing muffin tin
19 ounces (about 3¾ cups) bittersweet chocolate, finely chopped
12 tablespoons (1½ sticks) unsalted butter
8 large egg yolks
½ cup plus 2 tablespoons sugar
8 large egg whites
2 cups Caramel Sauce (page 249)
1 quart vanilla ice cream (optional)

1. Preheat the oven to 350°F. Spray an oversized muffin tin that holds 8 muffins with baking spray or prepare it with a thin coat of butter and flour.

2. Melt 15 ounces (3 cups) of the chocolate along with the butter in a microwave or double boiler. Remove from the heat and allow to cool to room temperature.

3. In an electric mixer (or in a large bowl with a whisk), beat the egg yolks until thick; add half of the sugar and continue beating until pale yellow.

4. In a separate, clean stainless-steel bowl, beat the egg whites with the remaining sugar until the whites hold soft peaks.

5. Fold the yolk mixture into the chocolate. Fold in the egg whites and the remaining 4 ounces (¾ cup) chocolate, being careful not to overmix.

6. Fill the muffin molds three-quarters full and bake until the tops are cracked and the chocolate is still oozing inside, about 35 minutes. Allow to cool slightly, and then unmold the cakes onto serving plates. Serve with caramel sauce and ice cream, if desired.

BEAUTY AND THE BEACH

When we decided to include a spa in our hotel, we turned to internationally renowned spa guru Ole Henriksen. Originally, the Denmark native was drawn to the energizing and healing powers of the Nordic Sea. Later, as a spa professional, he made the connection between the revitalizing energy of the ocean and restorative treatments, creating luxurious therapies centered around extracts such as sea salt, mineral-rich salt water, seaweed, and mud. As someone who has always looked to the beach for inspiration, he couldn't be a more perfect fit to oversee treatments at Shutters' ONE Spa. In the following pages, Ole graciously shares some easy beach-inspired home treatments so you can pamper yourself anytime. Should you choose to whip up a batch, make extra—each formulation can be stored in the refrigerator and used over several weeks.

Beach Body Scrub

The secret to making your skin baby smooth is in the natural ingredients of this deep-cleansing scrub: sea salt to retexture the skin, coffee beans to help firm the skin and fight cellulite, sesame oil to soften and nourish the skin, and eucalyptus oil to oxygenate and purify.

½ cup fine sea salt
½ cup finely ground coffee beans
½ cup sesame oil
½ teaspoon (about 20 drops) eucalyptus essential oil (see Source Guide)

makes 1 ½ cups, enough for 3 treatments

In a small bowl, mix the salt, coffee, and sesame and eucalyptus oils. Use the scrub in the shower while standing out of your showerhead's reach. Massage it into damp skin with long, firm, semicircular movements, taking time in order to activate the ingredients. Rinse well.

Scandinavian Rose Hips Face and Body Mist

This is a rejuvenating blend to bring along to the beach or any sunny destination. Rose hip tea is high in vitamin C and antioxidants, aloe vera is lightly hydrating and antiinflammatory, chamomile is calming and soothing, and lavender is known for its antiwrinkle and antiseptic benefits. If using the mist outdoors, store it in your ice chest for extra refreshment.

⅓ cup strongly brewed rose hip tea   makes 1 cup
⅓ cup aloe vera gel or juice
½ teaspoon (about 20 drops) lavender essential oil (see Source Guide)

Mix the ingredients together in a mister bottle that provides fine diffusion. Apply it at regular intervals while on the beach or at home, following face and body cleansing. You can spray it on top of water-resistant sun care products without diluting their SPF factor.

Ole's Age-Defying Complexion Scrub

This invigorating skin treatment combines salt to exfoliate, sugar to dislodge and dissolve dead skin cells, almond oil to smooth and nourish the skin, and lavender oil to discourage wrinkles.

2 tablespoons fine sea salt   makes ⅓ cup, enough for 2 treatments
2 tablespoons sugar
2 tablespoons almond oil
⅛ teaspoon (about 10 drops) lavender essential oil (see Source Guide)

Mix together the salt, sugar, and almond and lavender oils and store in a small covered glass jar. For best results, massage the scrub into damp skin in small upward and outward circular motions for 1 to 2 minutes. Repeat the treatment 2 or 3 times per week on clean skin to ensure better absorption of moisturizers and sun care products.

MISTYMORNINGS

Morning is a welcome friend or a necessary evil, depending on your mood. But pulling crisp white sheets up to your chin and dreaming of the day to come (or the previous evening) is a weekend indulgence few at our hotel can pass up.

This chapter will give you some wonderful recipes to coax you out of bed, from the perfect smoothie to our ever-popular breakfast dishes. Room service is a given luxury at Shutters, and breakfast is the most requested meal, arriving at guests' rooms with the gentlest of knocks. At home, breakfast in bed can be just as decadent; it just takes a little planning and a few exquisite details. A sturdy yet stylish wicker tray for presenting the morning meal, a carafe of freshly brewed coffee, elegant cups and saucers, pretty cloth napkins, and the morning newspaper are divine ways to welcome the day. With a few easy touches to the morning routine, you might find you actually look forward to seeing the sun come up.

MISTYMORNINGS

Mango-Papaya Smoothie

Strawberry-Orange Juice

Peach-Coconut Smoothie

Beach Granola

Granola, Vanilla Yogurt, and Wild Berry Parfait

Irish Oatmeal

Cranberry-Orange Pistachio Bread

Giant Walnut Sticky Buns

Raisin Brioche French Toast with Glazed Berries

Boardwalk Bran Muffins

Lemon-Ricotta Pancakes

Bull's-Eye Eggs

Asparagus–Egg White Omelet

Scrambled Eggs with Mushrooms and Oven-Dried Tomatoes

Frittata of Shrimp, Fontina, Tomato, and Basil

Breakfast Counter Potatoes

MANGO-PAPAYA SMOOTHIE

One way to brighten the morning is to whip up this creamy taste of the tropics.

1 cup milk (skim or low-fat is fine)
1 papaya, halved, seeded, peeled, and chopped
2 cups frozen mango
1 cup plain yogurt
2 tablespoons honey, or more to taste
Lime slices, for garnish

serves two to four

In a blender, liquefy the milk, papaya, and mango with ½ cup water until slushy. Add the yogurt and honey and blend well. Pour into chilled glasses. Garnish with slices of lime.

STRAWBERRY-ORANGE JUICE

A glass of this sunrise-colored juice is a refreshing variation on the morning classic.

1 cup fresh strawberries, hulled, plus extra for garnish
1 cup orange juice
2 cups ice cubes
1 tablespoon sugar
Whole strawberries, for garnish

serves two

In a blender, combine the strawberries, orange juice, ice cubes, and sugar. Blend until smooth. Pour into chilled glasses and garnish with fresh strawberries.

How to Make a Perfect Smoothie

Why serve an ordinary glass of orange juice when you can whip up a fresh smoothie in a matter of minutes? Here's how the bartender at Shutters' boardwalk café became famous for his smoothies, which we serve all day long:

1. Start with organic frozen fruit, slightly thawed. Frozen fruit often tastes slightly fresher than fresh because it has been flash-frozen at the peak of ripeness. It also blends into a smoother-textured smoothie. Try frozen mango, peaches, and berries. A ripe banana will add a silkier feel as well as natural sweetness.

2. Add a little water to each blender batch to facilitate blending. Or try coconut water (available at natural foods stores and Asian markets) for a tropical twist.

3. Do not use ice—you are not making a frozen margarita! Ice makes a smoothie lumpy and will cause it to separate as it sits.

4. Garnish each smoothie with a fresh strawberry (keep the green leaves on for color), slice of orange, or wedge of fruit.

PEACH-COCONUT SMOOTHIE

My favorite morning concoction, this creamy drink conjures up sweet memories of beach vacations. It tastes like a virgin peach piña colada with a California twist. Try making it with raspberries or pineapple if you prefer.

1 cup milk (nonfat or low-fat)
2 cups frozen peaches
1 cup sweetened shredded coconut
½ cup peach or coconut yogurt
Strawberries, for garnish

serves two to four

In a blender, liquefy the milk, peaches, and coconut with ½ cup water until slushy. Add the yogurt and blend well. Pour into chilled glasses. Garnish each with a strawberry.

BEACH GRANOLA

Making this wholesome, just-sweet-enough granola has become a regular Sunday-morning activity in our house. We make a double batch with the intention of enjoying it for the rest of the week, but I invariably end up packing it in pastel take-out boxes to give our friends as gourmet gifts. I like to boost the fiber by adding a cup of flaxseeds, bran, or bran flakes along with the oats. Once the granola is baked, you can jazz it up with diced dried apricots, dried blueberries, or other dried fruit of choice.

8 tablespoons (1 stick) unsalted butter
$\frac{1}{2}$ cup grapeseed oil
$\frac{1}{2}$ cup fresh orange juice
$\frac{1}{2}$ cup maple syrup
$1\frac{1}{4}$ cups packed brown sugar
$1\frac{1}{2}$ pounds oats (about $7\frac{1}{2}$ cups)
1 cup unsalted cashew pieces
1 cup sliced almonds
$\frac{1}{2}$ cup sunflower seeds
1 cup sweetened shredded coconut
1 tablespoon ground cinnamon
2 teaspoons ground nutmeg
1 cup dried cranberries

1. Preheat the oven to 275°F.

2. In a small saucepan, heat the butter, oil, orange juice, maple syrup, and brown sugar over medium-high heat, stirring occasionally until the sugar has dissolved.

3. In a large mixing bowl, mix the oats, cashews, almonds, sunflower seeds, coconut, cinnamon, and nutmeg. Toss the dry ingredients with the melted butter mixture and spread onto 2 baking sheets.

4. Bake until golden brown, stirring halfway through, about 1 hour. Remove from the oven and let cool completely. Mix in the dried cranberries. Store in resealable plastic bags or airtight containers.

GRANOLA, VANILLA YOGURT, AND WILD BERRY PARFAIT

For a refined brunch or a special breakfast, this smart presentation makes granola as irresistible as dessert. When fresh berries are in season, I take advantage by adding layers of raspberries, blueberries, and wild strawberries. In colder months, I use other fruit such as sliced bananas or cubes of fresh mango and papaya.

2 cups vanilla yogurt
2 cups Beach Granola (page 206)
2 cups fresh berries or fruit of your choice
4 tablespoons honey
4 sprigs fresh mint, for garnish

Line up 4 parfait, white wine, or other tall glasses. Place 2 tablespoons of yogurt in each glass. Spoon 2 tablespoons of granola on top of the yogurt. Spoon 2 tablespoons of fruit over the granola and drizzle with a little honey. Repeat the process to fill each glass. Garnish each parfait with a sprig of mint.

IRISH OATMEAL

serves two to four

Before you skip to a more exciting breakfast choice, consider this recipe for oatmeal, whose only similarity to the mushy gruel of my childhood is its stellar health benefits. Irish oats are steel-cut to preserve the chewy texture and natural flavor of the whole groats. The only catch is that to cook them adequately, you might have to roll out of bed a bit earlier than you'd like.

1 cup steel-cut Irish oats
4 cups water (substitute low-fat milk for a creamier texture)
Pinch of kosher salt
Raisins or dried blueberries, for garnish
Brown sugar or maple syrup, for serving

1. Combine the oats, water, and salt in a saucepan and let the oats soak for 15 minutes.

2. Bring to a boil over medium-high heat, then lower the heat and simmer slowly, stirring often. Cook until thickened and tender, 30 to 40 minutes.

3. Serve immediately, topped with raisins or dried blueberries, and with brown sugar or maple syrup on the side.

CRANBERRY-ORANGE PISTACHIO BREAD

makes one (9-inch) loaf

Years ago at our restaurant One Pico, every table of brunch guests was greeted with a basket filled with warm slices of this fragrant, delightfully speckled bread, along with a crock of creamy butter. But after spoiling too many appetites, the chefs decided to offer it by request only. Today, many regulars are in on the secret and ask for it as soon as they sit down!

Butter or baking spray, for preparing pan
2 cups all-purpose flour
1 cup sugar
1½ teaspoons double-acting baking powder
1 teaspoon kosher salt
½ teaspoon baking soda
8 tablespoons (1 stick) unsalted butter, chilled and cut into bits
1 teaspoon grated orange zest
¾ cup fresh orange juice
1 large egg
1 cup coarsely chopped dried cranberries
⅓ cup coarsely chopped unsalted pistachios or walnuts

1. Preheat the oven to 350°F. Butter a 9 × 5-inch loaf pan or coat it with baking spray.

2. In a food processor or in a bowl with a pastry blender, blend the flour, sugar, baking powder, salt, baking soda, and butter until the mixture resembles coarse meal; transfer the mixture to a large bowl.

3. In a small bowl, whisk together the orange zest, orange juice, and egg. Add to the flour mixture, and stir the batter until it is just combined. Stir in the cranberries and nuts.

4. Transfer the batter to the prepared loaf pan. Bake the bread until a tester comes out clean, about 1¼ hours. Let the bread cool in the pan for 15 minutes, then carefully remove it from the pan. Serve the bread warm, or, when it is completely cooled, slice, wrap in wax paper and aluminum foil, and freeze. Warm the slices in the oven before serving.

GIANT WALNUT STICKY BUNS

Sticky buns are one of those rare treats that we seem to indulge in only on special occasions or in airports. But there is nothing more mouthwatering than the aroma of sticky buns baking at home. This recipe will give you renewed confidence in making your own pastries, as it is quickly assembled and requires only an unsupervised hour for the buns to plump up and ready themselves for the oven. If you like them extra gooey, invert the pan as soon as you remove it from the oven and allow the caramel topping to seep down into the buns.

9 tablespoons (1 stick plus 1 tablespoon)
   unsalted butter, softened
½ cup packed golden brown sugar
¼ cup maple syrup, plus additional for brushing
1 cup chopped walnuts
½ cup raisins, optional

2 cups all-purpose flour, plus more if needed
1 package active dry yeast
¼ cup granulated sugar
¾ teaspoon kosher salt
⅔ cup warm water
2 large eggs

1. In a small saucepan over medium heat, melt 4 tablespoons of the butter. Add the brown sugar and maple syrup and heat, stirring, until the sugar has dissolved. Pour the mixture into the bottom of an 8-inch square pan. Sprinkle with ½ cup of the chopped walnuts and the raisins, if desired.

2. In a food processor or large mixing bowl, combine the flour, yeast, granulated sugar, and salt. Add the remaining 5 tablespoons butter and the ⅔ cup warm water. Beat for 2 minutes, scraping the bowl often with a spatula. Add the eggs and continue to beat for 2 more minutes. Stir in additional flour if needed to make a soft dough.

3. Turn the dough onto a lightly floured surface and knead it well, 8 to 10 minutes. Roll the dough into a 9-inch-wide rectangle, brush lightly with maple syrup, and sprinkle with the remaining ½ cup walnuts. Roll up into a 9-inch-long roll, pressing the seam well to seal it.

4. Slice the roll into six 1½-inch slices and place them cut side up in the prepared pan. Cover the pan lightly with plastic wrap and place the buns in a warm place to rise for about an hour.

5. Preheat the oven to 375°F.

6. Bake the buns until golden brown, 20 to 25 minutes. While the buns are still warm, use a knife to loosen them from the sides of the pan, then invert the whole pan onto a plate. Separate and serve the buns immediately, or let cool and then store them in an airtight container in the refrigerator for up to 2 days. Warm them in the oven before serving.

RAISIN BRIOCHE FRENCH TOAST
WITH GLAZED BERRIES

serves six

I like to spoil the kids with this treat on lazy weekend mornings. The trick to making decadent French toast like they do in hotels is to start with an unsliced loaf of cakelike egg bread, in this case raisin brioche (other good choices are challah or panettone). Slice the bread at least an inch thick so it will absorb all the custardy batter.

6 large eggs
1½ cups whole milk
½ teaspoon ground cinnamon, plus extra for serving
1 teaspoon vanilla extract

6 thick slices of raisin brioche
4 tablespoons unsalted butter
Confectioners' sugar, for serving
Glazed Berries (recipe follows) or 3 cups mixed fresh berries

1. In a small bowl, mix the eggs, milk, cinnamon, and vanilla. Place the bread in an even layer in a shallow dish and pour the egg mixture over it. Do this just before you are ready to cook the French toast.

2. Heat a large skillet over medium heat. Add the butter and cook until it begins to foam. Add the bread slices and cook on both sides until golden brown, about 3 minutes per side.

3. Sprinkle with cinnamon and confectioners' sugar. Serve topped with the berries.

GLAZED BERRIES

¼ cup sugar
2 tablespoons unsalted butter
4 teaspoons fresh lemon juice
1 teaspoon ground cinnamon

1 cup strawberries, rinsed and hulled
1 cup blackberries
1 cup raspberries

1. In a medium saucepan, combine the sugar, butter, lemon juice, and cinnamon. Cook, stirring over medium-low heat, until syrupy and thickened, about 2 minutes.

2. Remove from the heat and add the berries, tossing gently to coat. Serve warm, or cool and refrigerate until ready to serve.

BOARDWALK
BRAN MUFFINS

If bran muffins make you think of boring health food, think again. These are as moist as muffins come, despite the fact that they are full of fiber, low in fat, and devoid of white flour. While they bake, they will fill your kitchen with the toasty aromas of cinnamon and wholesome goodness. With just the right balance of sweetness and spice, they are delicious on their own or slathered with cream cheese or plain yogurt.

Baking spray, for preparing pan
1 cup oat bran
1¼ cups whole-wheat flour
⅓ cup packed brown sugar
2 teaspoons baking soda
½ teaspoon kosher salt
1 teaspoon ground cinnamon
½ cup grapeseed or canola oil
3 eggs
½ cup molasses
½ cup honey
1¼ cups buttermilk
½ cup dried blueberries or raisins

1. Preheat the oven to 375°F. Coat a muffin tray with baking spray or fill with muffin liners and set aside.

2. In a large bowl, mix together the oat bran, flour, sugar, baking soda, salt, and cinnamon.

3. In a separate bowl, combine the oil, eggs, molasses, and honey.

4. Add the wet ingredients into the dry ingredients and mix well. Pour in the buttermilk and mix thoroughly. The batter should be very fluid. Stir in the dried blueberries.

5. Fill the molds to the tops with batter. Bake until the muffins are puffed up and a tester inserted into the center comes out clean, 25 to 30 minutes. Unmold the muffins and transfer to a rack to cool. They will last up to a week when stored in an airtight bag in the refrigerator (warm them in the oven before serving).

LEMON-RICOTTA PANCAKES

makes 6 large pancakes; serves two to three

In case you are curious, this is it — Shutters' most requested recipe. There must be something irresistible about these remarkably light pancakes with a tangy whiff of lemon. The secret is to fold fluffy egg whites into the batter and not to overdo the sugar. I've been known to eat them for dinner. Fresh berries on the side add a splash of color. (See photograph, page 218.)

4 large egg yolks
¼ cup granulated sugar
2 teaspoons grated lemon zest
½ teaspoon lemon extract or lemon oil
¼ cup cake or all-purpose flour
Pinch of kosher salt
1 cup ricotta cheese
2 tablespoons unsalted butter, melted and cooled slightly
4 large egg whites
Canola oil or nonstick spray, for cooking
Confectioners' sugar, for serving
Maple syrup, for serving
Mixed berries, optional

1. In a medium bowl, combine the egg yolks, sugar, lemon zest, and lemon extract; whisk until light in color and aerated, about 2 minutes. Whisk in the flour and salt, then whisk in the ricotta cheese and melted butter until just incorporated.

2. In a separate bowl, whisk the egg whites to stiff peaks. Fold them into the batter, being careful not to overmix. The batter can be prepared the night before and refrigerated.

3. Heat a griddle or a large sauté pan over medium heat and coat it lightly with oil. Pour ½-cup circles of batter and cook until bubbles begin to form on the tops of the pancakes and the bottoms are golden, about 2 minutes. Then flip carefully and continue cooking until the pancakes are golden on the other side and dry in the middle.

4. Transfer the pancakes to serving plates and sprinkle with confectioners' sugar, or keep them warm in a 200°F oven until ready to serve. Serve with syrup and berries on the side.

HOW TO CAPTURE THE
BEACH VIBE
IN THE BEDROOM

You don't need an ocean view to create the kind of bedroom you can't wait to come home to. Take a cue from Shutters and make your sleeping space a destination in itself.

Though many homes now have a separate room for every need, a well-designed bedroom allows you to go from work to repose to sleep without leaving the room.

At Shutters, each guest room is designed to appeal to every whim, and comfort is the first priority. Across from the bed, there is a cozy armchair for reading, relaxing, or admiring the view, along with a garden stool for placing eyeglasses and a cup of tea. Barefoot-friendly floors; indoor shutters; soft, rounded furniture; and a roomy desk infuse the room with charming functionality.

Lighting is also important in creating a warm, breezy vibe. During the day when the shutters are pulled back, sunshine and fresh air illuminate the rooms. Once twilight falls, good overhead reading lights and subtle linen-covered lamps on either side of the beds are all that's needed for a little hotel luxury.

But most important is the bed, which may be just as talked about as our views. To create one worthy of lingering in, we rely on a firm pillow-top mattress, cotton Frette bed linens, a sumptuous quilt, and lots of fluffy pillows.

No matter where you reside, give your bedroom a beckoning beach allure, and make it a stylish place of refuge.

BULL'S-EYE EGGS

Whenever our family gathers for Sunday brunch at the hotel, we all end up ordering this: grilled eggplant slices with sunny-side-up eggs and a spicy tomato sauce flecked with slivers of garlic. The eggs are served in individual ceramic *cocottes,* or crocks, and can be prepared any way you like. This dish reminds me of the leisurely mornings I used to enjoy in my prechildren days!

1 small eggplant (about 6 ounces)
4 tablespoons extra-virgin olive oil
Kosher salt and freshly ground black pepper
4 large eggs
1 cup Spicy Tomato Sauce (page 247)

1. Preheat a grill pan over medium-high heat.

2. Cut the eggplant into 1-inch-thick slices. Brush them with 2 tablespoons of the olive oil, season generously with salt and pepper, and grill each side for about 5 minutes or until lightly charred. Remove from the heat and keep warm.

3. In a small nonstick pan, heat the remaining 2 tablespoons oil over medium heat. Add the eggs and cook sunny-side-up or to your liking. Season with salt and pepper.

4. To serve, place the grilled eggplant slices on warmed serving plates or in *cocottes* and pour the tomato sauce on top. Carefully slide the eggs over the sauce and serve immediately.

ASPARAGUS—
EGG WHITE OMELET

The trick to making an omelet look as if a professional made it is a well-oiled pan and adequately whipped egg whites. Add some diced vegetables from last night's dinner or your favorite cheese for extra kick. Serve it with fresh fruit, Breakfast Counter Potatoes (page 227), or a simple mixed green salad.

4 tablespoons extra-virgin olive oil
6 asparagus spears, tough ends trimmed, cut into ¼-inch pieces
Kosher salt and freshly ground black pepper
8 large egg whites
2 tablespoons chopped chives

1. In a small nonstick pan, heat 2 tablespoons of the oil over medium heat. Add the asparagus and cook, tossing gently, until tender but still crunchy. Season with salt and pepper and set aside.

2. In a medium bowl, beat the egg whites with a fork until frothy. Add the chives and season the mixture generously with salt and pepper.

3. Using the same nonstick pan, heat 1 tablespoon of the oil over medium-high heat. Pour half the egg-white mixture into the pan and, using a spatula, quickly draw the edges to the center so that the omelet cooks evenly. Reduce the heat and continue cooking until the egg whites are set but still creamy.

4. Spoon half of the asparagus in the center of the cooked egg whites and leave on the heat for a half minute or so longer. Using a spatula, fold the omelet toward one edge of the pan, giving the pan a light tap to loosen the omelet. Slide the omelet onto a warmed serving plate.

5. Repeat the process for the second omelet. Serve immediately.

SCRAMBLED EGGS
WITH MUSHROOMS AND
OVEN-DRIED TOMATOES

Instead of serving predictable scrambled eggs, try this jaunty version. If breakfast is upon you and you don't have oven-dried tomatoes on hand, use sun-dried tomatoes instead. Breakfast Counter Potatoes (page 227) are my favorite accompaniment.

4 large eggs
Kosher salt and freshly ground black pepper
2 tablespoons unsalted butter or olive oil
6 ounces white or cremini mushrooms, washed (see page 26) and sliced
8 pieces Oven-Dried Tomatoes (page 244), chopped

1. In a mixing bowl, beat the eggs with salt and pepper to taste until well blended.

2. In a medium nonstick pan, melt the butter over medium heat until bubbling. Add the mushrooms and sauté until their liquid has evaporated and they are golden.

3. Reduce the heat to medium-low and pour in the egg mixture. Using a spatula, stir constantly, scraping from the bottom and sides to achieve proper creaminess.

4. When the eggs begin to set, reduce the heat to low and add the tomatoes. Continue stirring and cooking to desired doneness. Turn onto warmed plates and serve immediately.

FRITTATA OF SHRIMP, FONTINA, TOMATO, AND BASIL

serves two to four

A frittata, or flat omelet, is prepared much like a regular omelet, except instead of completely cooking the eggs on the stove, they are finished in the oven. Just about any cooked vegetables can be tossed in with the eggs, and since the filling is distributed throughout, there is a shot of flavor in each bite. Instead of rock shrimp, you can substitute regular shrimp, imitation crab, vegetarian sausage, or soy bacon, chopped into bite-sized pieces.

1 tablespoon vegetable oil
½ cup chopped green bell pepper
½ medium yellow onion, chopped
2 garlic cloves, minced
½ teaspoon dried thyme
6 ounces peeled rock shrimp
6 large eggs
½ cup milk
2 tablespoons chopped fresh basil leaves
Kosher salt and freshly ground black pepper
1 plum tomato, seeded and diced
4 ounces grated Fontina cheese (½ cup)

1. Preheat the broiler.

2. In a large ovenproof skillet, heat the oil over medium heat and add the bell pepper, onion, garlic, and thyme. Cook, stirring occasionally, until the vegetables are tender, about 5 minutes. Add the rock shrimp and cook until pink, 2 minutes.

3. Meanwhile, in a small bowl, beat together the eggs, milk, and basil; season with salt and pepper. Pour over the shrimp-and-vegetable mixture. Reduce the heat to low and cook without stirring until the eggs are almost set, 6 to 8 minutes. Sprinkle the egg mixture with the tomato and Fontina cheese.

4. Transfer the skillet to the oven. Broil until the eggs are completely set and the cheese is melted and bubbling, 2 to 3 minutes.

5. Slice into wedges and serve immediately.

BREAKFAST COUNTER
POTATOES

Golden crusted and wickedly enticing, these potatoes are a crowd-pleaser that turns any egg dish into a feast. Patient cooking makes the potatoes crisp on the outside and creamy inside. Choose waxy potatoes that will hold their shape during cooking, such as Yukon gold, red bliss, or Peruvian purple. For more rustic appeal, leave the skins on the potatoes.

2 large potatoes, cut into ¾-inch cubes
1 medium yellow onion, chopped
4 tablespoons unsalted butter
Kosher salt and freshly ground black pepper
¼ cup chopped fresh flat-leaf parsley

1. Bring a large pot of salted water to a boil. Add the diced potatoes and cook until nearly tender but not fully cooked, about 10 minutes. Drain the potatoes, dry them with a kitchen towel, and toss them with the onions.

2. In a large, heavy skillet, melt the butter over medium heat. Add the potatoes and onions and cook until nicely and evenly browned, 25 to 30 minutes. Season to taste with salt and pepper, sprinkle with the parsley, and serve.

BEACH CHIC DÉCOR

Los Angeles' acclaimed interior designer Michael Smith knows a thing or two about breezy digs. Born and raised in Newport Beach, California, Michael built an international reputation creating interiors that integrate glamour and sophistication with hip informality. He deftly combines antiques with contemporary pieces, ethnic with all-American, and decorative elements with functional livability. The California part of Michael's aesthetic, as he explains it, comes as an innate sense of knowing when enough design is enough—when comfort, light, and soul come into play.

According to Smith, beach chic requires neither a beach nor a well-honed sense of chic, and it can be created in any room of the house. It goes beyond that casual California look that has become ubiquitous—slipcover couches, whitewashed floors, and flea-market finds. It is luxe with a light touch. No gimmicks, gilt, or expensive floral arrangements necessary. Instead, simple serenity is revered.

Creating a wonderful beach-inspired space starts with choosing the right wall colors. Keep in mind that trendy colors fall out of favor; save them for your wardrobe and stick with soft, saturated colors. At Shutters, Michael used a creamy vanilla paint for the guest-room walls, which diffuses the lovely apricot-colored Santa Monica light. A crisp, eggshell white sets off the architectural details of the bookshelves, moldings, and interior shutters. Michael also loves the visual interest achieved by wallpaper. He designed a subtle teal-colored pattern for the bathroom walls to complement the dark, variegated oak floors.

If you love color and pattern, incorporate some of your favorites into the fabrics, accessories, and floor coverings. Don't be timid—there is nothing more chic than confident personal style. For Shutters' guest rooms, Michael brought the spirit of the beach indoors with a palette of ocean blues and browns and accentuated them with a lively mix of stripes, chintzes, large checks, and exotic Indian patterns.

Make your décor anything but predictable. As Michael explains, a room that is too formal, too symmetrical, or too "correct" can feel uptight. Whimsical touches like a colorful set of juggling balls, a spinning desktop decision-maker, quirky art, and humorous books will remind you and your guests that interior design—and life—can be gloriously lighthearted.

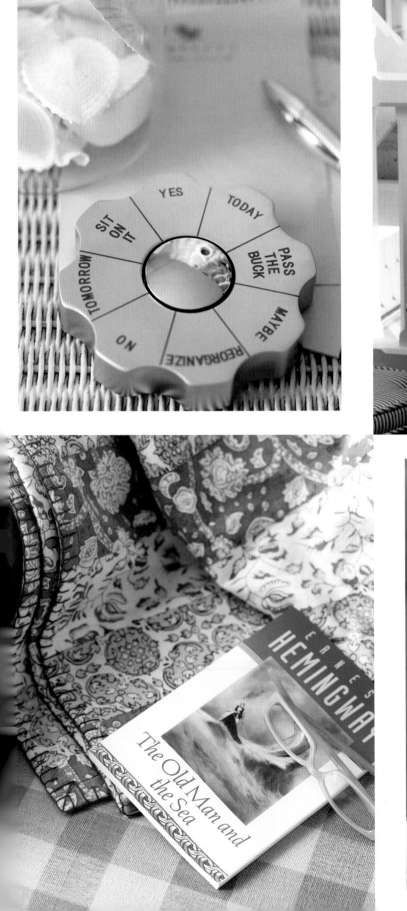

BEACHBASICS

The following recipes for sauces, condiments, vinaigrettes, and other accompaniments will take your cooking far beyond basic. Easy to make and essential to keep on hand for last-minute entertaining, they are used frequently throughout this book and are versatile enough to add a twist to your own favorite recipes.

Try one of the aïolis to spice up an ordinary sandwich, and experiment with the vinaigrettes to elevate any salad or grilled vegetables to gourmet heights. Check out the Roasted Garlic Olive Oil and Oven-Dried Tomatoes, and you might even develop a couple of new cravings.

When you're making one of these recipes, consider doubling it to have some on hand for future meals—or halving it if you are making a small meal and don't want leftovers.

All the following basics will keep well for up to one week, as long as they are stored in airtight containers in the back of your refrigerator.

BEACHBASICS

ROASTED GARLIC

A snap to prepare, roasted garlic can add depth and flavor to just about any dish that calls for garlic. For garlic fans, it is also delicious on its own, or spread on toasted bread or crackers.

1 head of garlic
Kosher salt and freshly ground black pepper
1 tablespoon extra-virgin olive oil

makes 6 to 8 cloves, or 1 head

1. Preheat the oven or a toaster oven to 400°F.

2. Slice off the top ½ inch of the garlic so that the cloves are partially exposed. Place the head of garlic on a square of aluminum foil. Sprinkle with salt and pepper and drizzle with the olive oil.

3. Wrap the garlic loosely in the foil and roast until the cloves squeeze out easily from their skins, about 1 hour.

4. Squeeze the cloves out of their skins into an airtight container. Store refrigerated for up to 1 week.

ROASTED GARLIC OLIVE OIL

I cook with this fragrant oil any time a recipe calls for oil and garlic — for salad dressings, pasta sauces, and quick sautéing of fish and vegetables. It eliminates the effort (and lingering odor) of peeling and mincing garlic cloves.

Roasted Garlic (above)
2 cups extra-virgin olive oil

makes 2 cups

Put the roasted garlic cloves in a glass bottle or airtight container. Fill with the oil and refrigerate for 1 day. Remove the garlic cloves (to prevent toxins from developing), seal the container tightly, and keep refrigerated for up to 2 weeks.

BASIC AÏOLI

Aïoli is a homemade mayonnaise with more pluck than usual thanks to a wink of garlic, citrus, and mustard. For the best results, start with room-temperature ingredients and utensils. Since raw egg yolk is required, make sure to use the freshest eggs and a clean bowl, and keep the aïoli well chilled once prepared. This recipe can easily be scaled up, in case you want to use the leftovers to top roasted potatoes or a simply grilled piece of fish.

1 large egg yolk
2 teaspoons fresh lemon juice
½ teaspoon Dijon mustard
2 small garlic cloves
Kosher salt
¼ cup extra-virgin olive oil
¼ cup vegetable oil
Freshly ground black pepper

makes ½ cup

1. Whisk together the yolk, lemon juice, and mustard in a medium bowl.

2. Mince and mash the garlic to a paste with a pinch of salt using a large, heavy knife; set aside.

3. Combine the olive and vegetable oils and add to the yolk mixture, a few drops at a time, whisking constantly until all the oil is incorporated and the mixture is emulsified.

4. Whisk in the garlic paste; season with salt and pepper to taste. Refrigerate until chilled before serving.

ROASTED PEPPER AÏOLI

This extra-piquant, blush-colored version of aïoli is delicious on any of the sandwiches in the "Sunny Days" chapter (pages 35–39), in Seaside Slaw (page 27), or as a dip for crudités.

1 cup Basic Aïoli (page 235) or mayonnaise
2 tablespoons puréed roasted red pepper (see page 136)
2 teaspoons minced yellow onion
1 teaspoon fresh lemon juice
1 teaspoon fresh lime juice
¼ teaspoon sugar
⅛ teaspoon kosher salt

makes 1 ¼ cups

In a small bowl, stir or whisk together the aïoli, red pepper, onion, lemon juice, lime juice, sugar, and salt to blend. Adjust seasoning to taste. Refrigerate until chilled before serving.

AVOCADO TARTAR SAUCE

With its gorgeous green hue and silky texture, this unusual sauce is another stellar sidekick for Dungeness Crab Cakes (page 40), burgers, and sandwiches. I like mine chunky, but if you prefer it smooth, mash the ingredients a little more.

½ cup mayonnaise
1 tablespoon chopped chives or scallion
1 teaspoon chopped fresh flat-leaf parsley
1 teaspoon chopped dill pickle
1 teaspoon fresh lemon juice
½ small avocado, peeled, pitted, and diced
Kosher salt and freshly ground black pepper

makes about ¾ cup

In a small bowl, using a fork, combine the mayonnaise, chives, parsley, pickle, lemon juice, avocado, and salt and pepper to taste; stir until incorporated, mashing the avocado for a smoother texture. Cover the surface with plastic wrap and refrigerate until chilled before serving.

CAPER RÉMOULADE

Like a chunky tartar sauce, this unabashedly gutsy condiment is superb alongside Grilled Turkey Burgers (page 134), Dungeness Crab Cakes (page 40), or grilled fish sandwiches. It's not bad on French fries, either!

¾ cup mayonnaise
1 tablespoon capers, rinsed and drained
2 garlic cloves, minced or pressed
1 tablespoon finely grated onion
Dash of Tabasco sauce
Kosher salt and freshly ground black pepper

makes about 1 cup

In a small bowl, combine the mayonnaise, capers, garlic, onion, Tabasco sauce, and salt and pepper to taste and whisk well. Refrigerate until chilled before serving.

BALSAMIC VINAIGRETTE

I enjoy experimenting with all the vinaigrettes in this chapter. Despite their distinctive flavors, they are practically interchangeable. But I always turn to this one for salads containing fruit or a bit of sweetness. It is also perfect for marinating vegetables to be grilled or roasted, as the sugars in the balsamic vinegar aid the vegetables in forming a delicious charred crust.

1 medium shallot, finely chopped
¼ cup balsamic vinegar
2 tablespoons sherry vinegar
½ teaspoon kosher salt
¼ teaspoon freshly ground black pepper
¾ cup extra-virgin olive oil
¼ cup grapeseed oil

makes 1¼ cups

In a medium bowl, combine the shallot, balsamic and sherry vinegars, salt, and pepper and whisk together. Whisk in the oils in a slow stream to emulsify. Adjust the seasoning to taste. Store refrigerated in an airtight container for up to 1 week.

FRESH HERB VINAIGRETTE

This bracing vinaigrette is at its best when fresh herbs are available, but if you have access to only dried varieties, by all means substitute them. I like to drizzle this dressing on salads that feature rich cheeses such as Stilton or Gorgonzola to balance and unite the flavors.

2 tablespoons white wine vinegar

makes 1 cup

¼ cup fresh lemon juice
2 tablespoons grated lemon zest
1 garlic clove
2 tablespoons chopped fresh herbs (such as parsley, basil, marjoram, and thyme)
2 teaspoons Dijon mustard
¾ cup extra-virgin olive oil
½ teaspoon kosher salt
Freshly ground black pepper

In a blender, combine the vinegar, lemon juice and zest, garlic, herbs, mustard, oil, salt, and pepper to taste; blend until emulsified. Adjust the seasoning to taste. Store refrigerated in an airtight container for up to 1 week.

RED WINE VINAIGRETTE

This flavorful vinaigrette adds spark to salad greens, especially those topped with grilled meat or chicken.

1 medium shallot, finely chopped

makes 1 cup

¼ cup red wine vinegar
2 tablespoons sherry vinegar
1 tablespoon Dijon mustard
½ teaspoon kosher salt
¼ teaspoon freshly ground black pepper
¾ cup grapeseed oil

In a medium bowl, whisk together the shallot, red wine and sherry vinegars, mustard, salt, and pepper. Whisk in the oil in a slow stream to emulsify. Adjust the seasoning to taste. Store refrigerated in an airtight container for up to 1 week.

LIME-MINT VINAIGRETTE

Try this perky vinaigrette on mild greens like frisée or butter lettuce. It can also double as a marinade for grilling fish, shrimp, and chicken.

¼ cup fresh lime juice

makes 1 ¼ cups

2 tablespoons champagne or white wine vinegar
¼ cup chopped fresh mint leaves
1 teaspoon Dijon mustard
1 small shallot, minced
1 small garlic clove, minced
¾ cup canola or grapeseed oil
Kosher salt and freshly ground black pepper

In a medium bowl, whisk together the lime juice, vinegar, mint, mustard, shallot, and garlic. Whisk in the oil in a slow stream to emulsify. Season to taste with salt and pepper. Store in an airtight container in the refrigerator for up to 1 week.

HONEY-TANGERINE VINAIGRETTE

This ambrosial vinaigrette is used in Dungeness Crab Salad (page 118), but it is also a sunny accompaniment to asparagus or delicate greens. Try pouring this vinaigrette over squash, root vegetables, or sweet potatoes before roasting them. If tangerines are not to be found, orange juice works just fine.

¼ cup honey

makes 1 ¼ cups

¼ cup fresh tangerine juice
1 small shallot, minced
1 small garlic clove, minced
1 teaspoon Dijon mustard
¾ cup canola oil
Kosher salt and freshly ground black pepper

In a medium bowl, whisk together the honey, tangerine juice, shallot, garlic, and mustard. Whisk in the oil in a slow stream to emulsify. Season to taste with salt and pepper. Store in an airtight container in the refrigerator for up to 1 week.

SHERRY VINAIGRETTE

More like a creamy sauce than a vinaigrette, this recipe is my favorite for salads that feature fish, such as Seared Tuna Salad Niçoise (page 30). Its slightly nutty flavor and velvety texture also complement bitter salad greens such as arugula, and salads featuring lentils, potatoes, or beets.

2 large eggs
1 medium shallot, finely chopped
2 tablespoons sherry vinegar
1 tablespoon Dijon mustard
¾ cup canola oil
Kosher salt and freshly ground black pepper

makes 1 cup

1. Bring a medium saucepan of water to a boil over medium-high heat. Gently add the eggs, reduce the heat, and simmer for 4 minutes. Drain, then run the eggs under cool water until cool enough to handle. Peel the eggs and reserve the yolks, saving the whites for another use.

2. In a small bowl, whisk together the yolks, shallot, vinegar, and mustard. Whisk in the oil in a slow stream to emulsify. Season with salt and pepper. Store in an airtight container in the refrigerator for up to 5 days.

OVEN-DRIED TOMATO VINAIGRETTE

Based on one of my favorite savory confections, this tangy, deep red vinaigrette has a caramel-like sweetness that goes well with Mediterranean Salad (page 115) and grilled meats, fish, and vegetables.

8 pieces Oven-Dried Tomatoes (page 244)
¼ cup balsamic vinegar, preferably white balsamic if available (see Source Guide)
¾ cup canola oil
1 teaspoon chopped fresh oregano leaves
Kosher salt and freshly ground black pepper

makes 1¼ cups

In a blender, blend together the tomatoes and vinegar until chunky but not puréed. With the blender running, slowly add the oil. Add the oregano and season to taste with salt and pepper. Store in an airtight container in the refrigerator for up to 1 week.

EGGLESS CAESAR DRESSING

I like to use this lightened version of Caesar dressing instead of the traditional egg-thickened recipe. It has just as much flavor, without the gluey consistency of most restaurant versions or the astringent bite of raw garlic. You will have no trouble evenly coating crisp romaine leaves with this healthy alternative. Now indulge guiltlessly with plenty of extra cheese!

2 teaspoons white wine or sherry vinegar
2 teaspoons fresh lemon juice
1 tablespoon Worcestershire sauce
1 teaspoon Dijon mustard
6 to 8 anchovy fillets packed in oil, drained
$\frac{1}{4}$ cup low-sodium vegetable or chicken broth
$\frac{1}{4}$ cup Roasted Garlic Olive Oil (page 234)
2 ounces soft tofu
$\frac{1}{4}$ cup freshly grated Parmesan cheese
Freshly ground black pepper

makes about $\frac{3}{4}$ cup

In a blender, combine the vinegar, lemon juice, Worcestershire sauce, mustard, anchovies, broth, oil, tofu, Parmesan cheese, and pepper to taste; blend until smooth. Adjust the seasoning if desired. Store in an airtight container in the refrigerator for up to 1 week.

LOUIE DRESSING

Whoever this Louie chap was, I love his dressing for many reasons, not the least of which is its endearing name. Chunky and sweet, it gets my vote as the ideal choice for Shutters Chopped Salad (page 26) and for spreading on sandwiches.

1 cup mayonnaise

¼ cup chili sauce or ketchup

1 hard-boiled egg, chopped

2 tablespoons finely chopped pimento-stuffed green olives

2 tablespoons sweet pickle relish, or more to taste

1 tablespoon grated onion

Juice of ½ lemon, or more to taste

Kosher salt and freshly ground black pepper

makes 1 ½ cups

In a medium bowl, combine the mayonnaise, chili sauce, egg, olives, relish, onion, lemon juice, and salt and pepper to taste; mix well. Add more pickle relish or lemon juice as desired. Store in an airtight container in the refrigerator for up to 1 week.

OVEN-DRIED TOMATOES

If you become as addicted to these tomatoes as I am, you will find umpteen tasty ways of using them. In egg dishes, quiches, salads, pastas, couscous, and rice, these intensely flavored tomatoes add great color, texture, and verve. Try putting them on little skewers or toothpicks along with bite-sized bocconcini (mozzarella) for a quick hors d'oeuvre. They also make a healthy snack. In our house, they barely make it to the refrigerator.

20 firm but ripe plum tomatoes (about 5 pounds)
¼ cup extra-virgin olive oil
2 tablespoons balsamic vinegar
2 tablespoons finely chopped fresh flat-leaf parsley or 1 tablespoon dried thyme
Kosher salt and freshly ground black pepper

1. Trim the stem ends off the tomatoes, quarter them lengthwise, and remove and discard the seeds.

2. Place the tomatoes in a large, nonreactive bowl and add the olive oil, vinegar, and parsley or dried thyme; mix well. Season the tomatoes generously with salt and pepper.

3. Preheat the oven to 200°F, preferably on convection heat if possible.

4. Arrange the tomatoes in a single layer on a nonstick baking sheet and bake for 3 hours, or until all the liquids have evaporated and the tomatoes are shriveled and dark on the edges but still rosy. (Alternatively, bake the tomatoes at 120°F overnight for 10 to 12 hours.)

5. To store, place the dried tomatoes in glass jars, seal tightly, and store refrigerated for up to 1 week. To store them for longer, cover them with olive oil and keep at room temperature for up to 2 weeks.

SPICY TOMATO SAUCE

This sauce is what makes our Bull's-Eye Eggs (page 220) so tempting. You can also add it to pastas, sausages, or, as I like to do for dinner parties, grilled whitefish—with niçoise olives and capers stirred in and Steamed Broccoli Rabe (page 183) on the side. Make it as spicy as you can handle.

3 tablespoons extra-virgin olive oil
½ large yellow onion, chopped
3 large garlic cloves, thinly sliced
1 (15-ounce) can diced Italian plum tomatoes with juice
1 (6-ounce) can tomato paste
½ cup dry red wine
1 teaspoon dried oregano
1 teaspoon dried basil
½ teaspoon red pepper flakes, or to taste
Kosher salt and freshly ground black pepper

1. In a medium sauté pan, heat the oil over medium heat. Add the onion and cook, stirring often, until softened, about 5 minutes. Add the garlic and continue cooking and stirring until the onion and garlic begin to caramelize, about 4 minutes.

2. Stir in the tomatoes, tomato paste, wine, oregano, and basil. Bring to a simmer and then cook, uncovered, until thickened, 10 to 15 minutes. Season to taste with red pepper flakes, salt, and pepper.

3. Serve immediately, or cool completely and refrigerate for up to 1 week or freeze in an airtight container for up to 3 months.

CHOCOLATE
PIECRUST

makes 2 (9-inch) pie shells

If you need a great reason to make crust from scratch, here it is: chocolate! Made with crunchy cocoa nibs, this bittersweet crust can elevate any number of desserts, including Malted Chocolate Cream Pie (page 98) or a chocolate pecan pie. You can also make edible cups for mousses or puddings by baking this in muffin molds instead of pie tins.

1 cup (2 sticks) unsalted butter, softened
1¼ cups sugar
2 large eggs
1¾ cups all-purpose flour
1 cup cocoa powder
1 teaspoon kosher salt
⅓ cup cocoa nibs (see Note)

1. In a food processor or mixer, combine the butter with the sugar and beat until creamy. Add the eggs one at a time.

2. In a separate bowl, whisk together the flour, cocoa powder, and salt. Add it to the butter mixture. Mix until just incorporated, and then fold in the cocoa nibs by hand.

3. On a floured surface, gather and gently press the dough into 2 disks. Wrap each in plastic and refrigerate for at least 1 hour or up to 3 days, or freeze for up to 2 months. When ready to use, remove the plastic wrap and allow the dough to thaw until it is pliable but still cold.

4. Roll out one of the disks of dough ⅛ inch thick and fit it into a 9-inch tart pan with a removable bottom, trimming any overhanging dough with scissors or a sharp knife. Prick the crust well with the tines of a fork and refrigerate for 24 hours or freeze for 1 hour.

5. To prebake the piecrust, preheat the oven 350°F. Bake the crust for 15 minutes or until set. Allow to cool before filling.

NOTE
Cocoa nibs are crunchy bits of roasted cocoa beans that burst with the essence of chocolate. A great substitute for roasted nuts or chocolate chips in many baked goods, they are available at gourmet stores and online (see Source Guide). If you can't find them, use chopped bittersweet chocolate chips instead.

CARAMEL
SAUCE

You don't have to be a pastry chef to pull off this rich and delicious sauce. Serve it with a slice of Apple-Jack Pie (page 187), Warm Pineapple Upside-Down Cake (page 194), Classic Chocolate Pudding Cakes (page 197), or a scoop of your favorite ice cream. I like to sprinkle the sauce with a few grains of sea salt for a beach twist. It will keep refrigerated for up to 2 weeks and can be reheated in the microwave.

1 cup light corn syrup
2 cups sugar
1 cup heavy cream
4 tablespoons (½ stick) unsalted butter

1. In a saucepan over medium heat, combine the corn syrup, sugar, and ½ cup water. Stir with a wooden spoon, and then cook without stirring until the mixture turns a light copper color, 15 to 20 minutes. Turn off the heat.

2. Immediately and carefully add the cream and butter (the mixture will splatter). Let the bubbling subside, and then stir to combine. Pour the sauce into a metal bowl to cool slightly. Serve immediately, or cool completely and refrigerate in an airtight container for up to 2 weeks.

ACKNOWLEDGMENTS

Like any memorable feast, this book would not have been created without the help and support of a multitude. My deepest gratitude goes to my husband, Edward, who was the very first to green-light my idea and, amazingly, is still rooting for me. Countless thank-yous also go to my agent and friend Elisabeth Weed, who cheerfully navigated this neophyte through the process from beginning to end; my editor, Rica Allannic at Clarkson Potter, who saw the diamond in the rough and painstakingly crafted it into a keeper; my dear brother, David, attorney extraordinaire and beloved compatriot; brother-in-law Tommy for enthusiastically signing on; the affably unflappable Dan Strone at Trident; style maven and mentor Andrea King; Klaus Mennekes and Tim Dubois, the dynamic and meticulous duo; Michael Smith and Ole Henriksen for lending their expertise; and the chefs and staff at Shutters for helping me share the recipes and style that best convey the spirit of our hotel.

Top credits and infinite gratitude go to delightful writer and friend Erika Lenkert, who helped me find my voice and also tested many recipes; talented photographer Amy Neunsinger and her amazing team, including Val Aikman-Smith, the food stylist; and creative director of Clarkson Potter Marysarah Quinn. I am truly indebted to you all for believing in me, in this book, and in everything beach chic.

Heaps of thank-yous to Dana Goodyear for her invaluable advice; Maryl Georgi for her groovy playlist suggestions; Chantel Kaufman for her floral artistry; and my dearest gal pals (you know who you are) for all the pep talks.

Much appreciation goes to my infinitely lovable and loving children—Audrey, Blake, and Cary—for their precious patience and hugs.

The following people were trusty recipe testers: Erika Lenkert, Nicole Hausman, Kirstie Payne, Edith Gautschi, Maxine Greenspan, Regina Pally, Darcy Pollack, Michelle Ratkovitch, and Rebecca Soliz.

Special thanks to all of the stores that so kindly lent their dazzling tableware for the photographs: Amen Wardy, Anthropologie, Barneys, Embrey Papers, and Neiman Marcus. Be sure to check out their websites (see Source Guide).

And, of course, thank you, readers, for making room on your shelves for another cookbook. I hope these pages bring about many delicious moments and rewarding adventures. Perhaps we can all help to heal this world one meal at a time.

SOURCEGUIDE

The following list of suppliers is limited to simply my personal favorites, where you easily can find some of the ingredients and items mentioned in this book.

Specialty Foods

The Beverly Hills Cheese Shoppe

www.cheesestorebh.com

Cheeses and specialty foods from all around the world, including Cotswolds, mascarpone, crème fraîche, Antonio Marella and Rustichetta d'Abruzzo pappardelle and other hand-cut pastas, Arborio and Carnaroli rice, pearl pasta, white balsamic vinegar, and anchovy-stuffed olives.

Chef Ming Tsai

www.ming.com

Well-designed online store specializing in Asian ingredients — fermented black beans, sake, mirin, hoisin sauce — plus cooking utensils and gifts.

Dean and Deluca

www.deandeluca.com

A Manhattan gourmet institution, which carries quail eggs, specialty oils, salts, dried mushrooms, premium chocolate, pomegranate syrup, rose water, beans, cheese, pasta, and the finest quality ingredients.

Kalustyan's

www.kalustyans.com

Exceptional online supplier of hard-to-find ingredients, such as gigante beans, pomegranate syrup, rose water, truffle oil, and eucalyptus and lavender essential oils.

Surfas

www.surfasonline.com

Culver City restaurant-supply and specialty-foods warehouse featuring wholesale pricing. Products include grapeseed oil, pearl pasta, white balsamic vinegar, saffron, vanilla bean, smoked salt, four-peppercorn blend, dried mushrooms, Horlicks malt powder, premium chocolate, cocoa nibs, passion fruit purée, pomegranate syrup, rose water, flavored wooden skewers, frozen piecrust, and many more.

Trader Joe's

www.traderjoes.com

National grocery chain that carries excellent organic, vegetarian, and kosher items, including prepared broths in cartons, low-sugar jams, frozen mango, frozen peaches, frozen roasted corn, jarred roasted peppers, prepared pesto, and frozen piecrusts.

Tableware and Home Accessories

Amen Wardy

www.amenwardyaspen.com

Fabulous Aspen-based retail store and online resource for beautiful serving pieces, table linens, candles, cocktail glasses and skewers, and specialty foods.

Anthropologie

www.anthropologie.com

A popular national retailer featuring an eclectic array of clothing and home items with a funky global vibe, including plates and glassware, candles and holders, pillows, blankets, and some kitchen supplies.

Barneys New York

www.barneys.com

Upscale purveyor of all things hip and chic, including home accessories, fine tableware, and decorative objects made by renowned artisans.

Crate and Barrel

www.crateandbarrel.com

National supplier of well-designed items for all areas of the home, including picnic baskets, blankets, serving pieces, cocktail glasses, scented linen sprays such as lavender water, and kitchen supplies.

Embrey Papers

www.embreypapers.com

A charming Brentwood boutique offering pretty items for the home as well as stationery and paper goods.

Neiman Marcus

www.neimanmarcus.com

High-end department stores offering beautiful china, flatware, and serving pieces, as well as fine chocolates.

Target

www.target.com

Ubiquitous megastores that carry seasonal selections of contemporary, well-priced items for everyday living and entertaining.

Note: Page numbers in *italics* refer to photographs.